I0428878

Refugee Story

Introduction

Middle east, is a mysterious world for many Europeans, when Middle east is mentioned all thoughts tend to think that it is a primitive world, there are no female human rights, full of wars and extremism, there is no one knows the real people there and how they live. There are many educated people there who follow the world news and their young males and females love and befriend each other like in Europe, but in hidden ways, because of the Islamic culture and rules, lives always find a way, the sex instinct exists everywhere and the young males there try to satisfy it with the opportunities available to them regardless of all the difficult conditions that their governments create like wars and economical crisis, still life goes on. The period which I will speak about is between (1961 – 1993) where there were no modern technology like the Internet, YouTube, twitter or mobile phones, only simple ways of communications like typical landline phones and writing letters and through that people get introduced and talk to each other and use TVs to follow the world news. The story shows a view on the bloody Iraq-Iran war which lasted for eight years and claimed one million lives and a view on the first gulf war, it is the story of a man who was born in a country full of violent political events and cut his way in life by leaving his native country in Iraq to Jordan then to Yemen and finally to settle in a foreign country to him England searching for safety and peace.

This story is dedicated to my friend at my present work Adam Green and my wife Lorraine for their encouragement for me to write it and for my mother Fareda for her continuous encouragement for me to write stories since childhood.

Childhood

Chapter 1

Shawkey was born in a poor area called (ALTOPCHY) in Baghdad capital of Iraq, in an area where most of the people have low incomes and have many children in spite of their poverty, the average number of children for house hold were (4-5) and the level of education was medium, their work between ordinary officers working in government institutions, workers in factories or mechanics. The area consist of medium size houses have (1-2) bedrooms and the rooms were crowded, Shawkey's house consisted of a room for guests, two bedrooms, kitchen and bathroom, all houses had open roof like all middle east style homes where the people used it to sleep on it in the summer nights where the weather becomes very hot to enjoy the cool breeze. In front of Shawkey's house there was a large piece of ground was build on it the electricity company which provided the area with electricity and beside it was build a secondary school and after some years a community clinic was built to treat the area people. The area streets were tarmac and there were sewer channels in the middle of the streets to carry the filthy water to the drainage holes, the houses were stuck to each other where you can hear your neighbour sounds through the wall if they were shouting or high TV volume. Shawkey's mother her name (Samera) met his father (Karem) when they were studying together at the Languages college, his father did not finish his college and joined the army as reserved officer then he convinced Samera to leave her college to get married and the result Karem became an army officer and Samera got a job as an accountant in a governmental company, generally the income of the family was medium, but higher than their neighbours and the entire street. Shawkey's father came from AL-HAKEM family which was a well known family in Iraq and had branches in Baghdad and Alnajaf which was a holy town in Iraq, Shawkey's father family belongs to the branch in Baghdad which was a rich family, but through the years it wasted its wealth on gambling and horse racing, therefore Karem did not inherent any wealth. Shawkey's mother came from Alnajaf town and also it was a wealthy family, but Samera did not inherent any money, because her relatives made a conspiracy to murder her father when she was a child so that he does not inherit the wealth of his father and according the Iraqi old rule the female children cannot inherent the wealth of their families, therefore Samera did not inherent any money, too. Shawkey was the first child to Samera and Karem, his neighbour on the right had five children and called ABO ADEL house for his oldest son ADEL and on the left his neighbour was called ABO FAESAL house they had two children the oldest one called FAESAL, then at the end of the street there was ABO NAWAL house they had six children, the oldest called NAWAL and she was a female. When Shawkey was (2-3) years old he used to sit in the garden alone and play by himself, he used to cut the leaves of the trees and imagine they are characters and start tell himself a story imagining that one of the leaves was the hero who fights the enemies (the other leaves) and imagine how he stabs one of them by making a hole in the leaf and he got injured by making a line on the hero leaf, then he rides his horse (a branch of a tree) and follow the evils to kill them, he used to make small holes in the ground where he hides from the evils then he surprises them and get in a dual with them using his sword to kill them, he used to spend long hours in the garden telling himself these stories and was enjoying it in his own little world. After two years from his birth, his sister (SAMA) was born to fill some of his loneliness, with the time passing and Shawkey got older there were times he needed to play with boys in his age, his favourite games were marbles and spinning top, the problem was that his neighbours children were jealous from him because his family income was higher that their parent's and Shawkey's parents can buy him what he liked and their parents cannot, and therefore after they play with him they beat him up, Shawkey used to play with a boy his name was EHSAN and he was in a similar age to Shawkey from ABO ADEL house, he used to play with him marble, if Shawkey lose there was no problem, but if he wins EHSAN would beat him and run away supported by his several brothers, then Samera starts complaining to Ehsan mother about her son aggression, he gets some criticism and case over in the second day Shawkey starts playing with Ehsan or another boy, in most cases the games finish peacefully , but the few times that ended with Shawkey been beaten had left deep scars in his memory for ever. Cowboy films were favourite to Shawkey, Karem used to take him and his sister Sama to the cinema to see them and as usual Shawkey used to make stories to himself, but this time he involved Sama with him, he gives her a toy revolver and he carries one himself then he teaches her how to stand in front of him for a dual and when he shoots his revolver which makes a sound he teaches her how to fall down, then both of them rides their horses (riding the pillows) and if his sister was not their he calls Ehsan or Samer from ABO NAWAL house to play cowboys with him, in all cases Shawkey was the writer, director of these games. When Shawkey reached age three years, his father wanted to circumcise him, that day Shawkey saw Karem and another man in the house, he did not know the reason and, when the time came for circumcision and saw the man carrying a knife and approaching him he run away from him, but Karem and the man run after him and he was cornered in a corner in the house and circumcised him, at that time Shawkey was crying from pain in spite of the reassuring talk from his father that everything will be alright. Part of the problems that Shawkey faced when he was three years old he got Asthma and that was a worry matter to his parents, his food apatite was reduced, but he used to drink a lot of milk and because of his condition he had to take injections , Samera used to take him weekly to her neighbour ABO NAWAL where his wife was a nurse, because of the amount of the needles he was injected with, he hated them and sometimes he used to run away to the street, which cause his mother Samera to run after him and bring him back to take the injection, this Asthma continued with Shawkey till he got to the age of six and then it disappeared and his appetite for food increased which made his parents happy and started giving him much food which made him fat.

Shawkey's mother raised him on restricted Islamic rules, she used to tell him if you do something bad you will go to hell and if you do something good you will go to heaven, so since childhood Shawkey's mentality was fed with this principal afraid to do anything bad and from her words to him (if you see someone eating shit will you eat shit), so that he do not do something wrong if he sees another person do it, like lying or stealing. Because of life difficulties, Samera and Karem were both working as accountants in government companies, his father had finished his military reserved service, and because both Shawkey and Sama were still children Samera wanted to employ a servant at home to look after the children and cleaning while she was at work, so Samera and Karem went to a house in a neighbouring area when they knew that the owners of the house wanted their daughter to work as a servant in other houses to earn some money, Samera spoke with the parents of the girl who her name was Sadeat and agreed with them about the working hours, Sadeat was fourteen years old, brown, had long black hair and black eyes, Shawkey was four years old and Sama two years old. The first week of her work finished without any incident, in the second week while Sadeat was playing with Shawkey and Sama on the bed in the bedroom, Shawkey pushed Sadeat on the bed and she fell on her back, then Shawkey told Sama to sit on her (as part of the game) , Sama sat on Sadeat chest, Sadeat was wearing a dress cover her body to her knees and knickers, when she fell on the bed her dress lifted to her upper thigh and the game was to prevent Sadeat from getting up, Shawkey sat on her left leg and Sama holding her right hand and sitting on her chest and every one were laughing, suddenly Shawkey pushed his first and middle fingers into Sadeat knickers , then he pushed his finger in her vagina and start moving it there, at that time Sadeat was not showing any resistant (although she was able to move Shawkey and Sama from top of her), after some time of moving Shawkey's finger inside Sadeat, Shawkey felt his fingers became wet and Sadeat resistant even got lesser and started making strange sounds like moans and because Shawkey was thinking that he and his sister had succeeded and got victory in the game, he continued to move his fingers inside Sadeat vagina and she became very wet, then after some quietness Sadeat raised and sat on the bed, she told Shawkey and Sama not to tell their parents of what happened otherwise there will be no more playing the game, Shawkey did not understand why he should not tell his parents about what happened , was there something happened and because Shawkey must tell his mother about everything happen in his day to make sure that he did not make anything bad which may lead him to hell, he was worried why Sadeat told him that. When his parents came back from work, Shawkey was worried will he tell his mother about what happened or not, but when his mother asked him about his day, Shawkey was embarrassed and told his mother about what happened and when he reached the part concerning his fingers and that he put his fingers in her knickers, his mother was exploded in anger and told him that was a very bad thing to do and he will go to hell. Shawkey starts crying severely and telling his mother (I do not want to go to hell, I want to go to heaven), but no use his mother was not replying to him, he kept on crying and after quarter an hour his mother told him that what he done was very wrong and he should not do it again, Shawkey told her that he will not do it again ever, then he asked her (will I go to hell) she answered (no, you will go to heaven) and he relaxed. Samera told Karem of what happened and in the same evening they took Shawkey and Sama to Sadeat parent's house and told them that they do not need Sadeat anymore because they found another person, but they did not tell them of what happened in the morning to prevent their anger on their daughter.

At Shawkey's street some houses their owners put big rocks in front of the house to sit on it in the summer evenings to chat with their neighbours, once Shawkey was playing football with his neighbours children, during the game the ball went to ABO FASEL house, Shawkey run after it and in order to catch it before someone else do he jumped over the rock, but he tripped and fall on the tarmac street, his point of contact with ground was on his front teeth, at that time Shawkey saw a white thing jump in front of his face, when he stood up he found that the white thing was a half tooth, he licked his front teeth and felt some pain, when he went back to home and saw the mirror, he found that half of his front middle tooth was missing, then his father told him that the tooth needs to be taken out, because it will cause him problems in the future, in the second day Karem took him to a dentist and took it out, which left a space between the front teeth, but with the years passing the gap was reduced and became a small gap.

Chapter 2

Shawkey's family life was not free from domestic violence, his father used to go to work in the morning and when he comes back in the afternoon he usually takes a nap when it is hot outside, he awakes in the evening and go out to the café which was not far from home, he spends (3-4) hours there playing backgammon with his friends then he comes back home, sometimes he brings with him Iraqi alcoholic drink called (ARAK) which was very alcohol concentrated drink, he drinks from it till he becomes drunk and sleeps. Once Shawkey was playing in the garden and his father was taking his usual nap, Shawkey entered the house and started hitting one of his toys which he was bored from it, this sound awoke his father, he was angry, he came and hit Shawkey on the back of his head, because of the strength of the hit his face hit the edge of the hand wash basin which led to cut his upper lip and bleed, Shawkey was in a lot of pain, Samera started arguing with Karem for his behaviour and telling him that Shawkey was only a child, but Shawkey learned his lesson and never made sounds again when Karem was sleeping. In another incident when his father returned from the café and started drinking ARAK he became drunk, there was an argument between him and Samera, he hit Samera with his hand and leg badly which made her crying and told her to leave the house, Samera took Shawkey and Sama and went to relatives of her in another part of Baghdad, her face was swollen, they let her and the children to stay with them till they speak with Karem about his vicious behaviour and forced him to apologise to Samera, so that she go back and stay with him, Karem came to their home and apologised to Samera, then she agreed to go back with him to home. When Shawkey was five years old and according to the restrict Islamic rules that his mother told him, he used to pray five times a day and go to the mosque to listen to the speeches of the Imam (which was the religious figure in the mosque who give speeches to all the worshipper), but Shawkey never understood why the Emam was always angry when he gives his speech and why always was shouting like all the worshippers were deaf, any way at that time the BA'ATH party took control of Iraq and AHMED AL-BAKR was the president of Iraq and his deputy was Saddam Hussein, this Ba'ath party started a crackdown campaign and arresting the members of all other political parties in Iraq including AL-DAWA party which was an Islamic party and making arrests to many mosques worshippers searching for its members, because they were afraid that these members may cause difficulties for them to govern Iraq, Samera told Shawkey to stop going to the mosque because she was afraid that he might be arrested by the security forces although he was a child and have no understanding of any politics, still going to the mosque was enough for him to be arrested.

One of Shawkey's favourite games was flying kites, he learned it from Karem, when he was four years old Karem made a kite for Shawkey and took him to the roof of the house and started flying it till it got high enough in the sky, then he gave the thread to Shawkey to control it and move it left or right and because they were living in a common area there were many children and even teenagers using kites as a hobby to pass time it was a cheap game to play, so there were many kites flying in the sky specially in the days where there was winds. One day while Shawkey was flying his kite there was a red kite flying near his white kite, suddenly the red kite started flying in his kite direction and getting nearer and nearer, the matter was not clear at that time to Shawkey and Karem why this was happening, so Karem told Shawkey to keep flying his kite and try to be away from the red kite to avoid tangle the two threads of the kites, but the red kite kept on moving towards the white one, then suddenly the red kite made a manoeuvre and its thread rubbed the white kite thread, at that time the white kite thread was cut and Shawkey's kite started flying away in the sky until it was lost, Shawkey did not know what happened , but Karem told him that the owner of the red kite has a stronger thread and possibly thread mixed with glass and that was the reason why their thread was cut , that was intention to cut other people threads and the process of cutting other people threads called (KASS), he use to play this games when he was a child visiting his relatives in KARBALA (which was a holly city in the south of Iraq). Shawkey became sad and started crying because he lost his kite, Karem told him to stop crying he will make another kite for him and this time he will make a glass thread (thread mixed with glass) for him and teach him how to do it. In the next day Karem brought with him after work a thread thicker than the one that they used in the previous time, then took a thin glass bulb and started crashing it using a manual crasher until he made it like wheat, then he started to funnel it through a female stocking to use the very thin glass, then he brought half cooked rice which was very sticky and started mixing it with the tiny glass, then he took the thick thread and tied it to a branch of a tree then across the garden and move it around another branch and came back to the original branch and move the thread around it and continued to the other branch and so on, while doing that he was moving the mixture of the rice and glass over the thread to make it soaked with the mixture, he made a glass thread for about sixty metres long, that was enough because this length will be at the near side of the kite where all the rubbing will occur, after that length a normal thread can be used. After doing first coat of the glass on the thread he let the thread to dry then he made another coat to it, then he left the thread to dry for three hours, then he started untie the thread and round it around a small cylindrical piece of plastic and tie it to the normal thread which does not have the glass mixture and told Shawkey that this time we will do the cutting not the owner of the red kite. In the evening when the sun temperature became bearable Karem and Shawkey went to the roof, there were many kites in the sky as usual, but the red kite was not there, Karem told Shawkey never mind we will cut him in another day, we need today to try our thread to see if it will do the job with other kites. Karem started flying a blue kite which he made earlier until it was flying high in the sky and gave the thread to Shawkey and told him to be careful when rewinding the thread when he finishes flying the kite to avoid cutting his hand with the glass thread. Shawkey continued to fly his kite then he noticed a green kite flying near his kite, he asked Karem if he can try to cut the thread of that kite, Karem agreed and helped Shawkey to steer his kite towards the green kite, when the blue kite became near the green one Karem took the thread and made a manoeuvre to steer the blue kite thread towards the green one thread and the rubbing happened between the threads and here we go the green kite thread was cut, the kite started flying away in the sky until it disappeared. Shawkey was very happy he knows now that he has a strong thread and no one can cut it, he wished that he see the red kite again, it was personal now. Three days past and there was no sign of the red kite, but in the fourth day while Shawkey and Karem were flying their blue kite the red kite appeared in the sky, but it was far from them, still the owner of the red kite started steering his kites towards Shawkey's one, in turn Karem started steering his kite towards the red one, after some time both kites were near each other, at that time the red kite made its manoeuvre to make contact between the threads, the contact occurred at that time Karem started to pull his thread fast to rub the thread of the red kite, nothing happened and both threads were intact, then he tried again to pull the thread fast to rub the thread of the red kite more and more and here we go the process was successful and the red kite thread was cut, the red kite started flying away in the sky till it was disappeared, Shawkey was jumping from joy and laughing, Karem was happy because he saw his son jumping from joy and laughed. Karem told Shawkey that he thinks that the owner of the red kite had a thick thread like them that was the reason why we could not cut it from the first attempt.

Because the difficult conditions of Shawkey playing in the street with his neighbours children where some times he comes back crying because they beat him, Samera wanted to keep him busy in something more useful to him, so when he became five years old he could not enrol in the primary governmental schools, she enrolled him in a Christian primary school called (NAGMAT ALSABAH) which means (the star of dawn), it was a primary schools run by sisters and accept children from the age of five. It was a successful experiment, because Shawkey from five years old learned the English alphabet, their way of teaching the letters was very easy by make him pronounce it in a musical tune, Shawkey learned the English alphabet by heart for ever and learned other English words, through one year Shawkey learned many information through the different lessons he took there which helped him in his future education.

When Shawkey became six years old Samera enrolled him in (ALMADRAST ALNAMOTHAGEAT) which means (the perfect school) primary school , it was one of the best governmental primary schools in Baghdad, his parents wanted him to get the best education regardless of the distance from home, recently the head teacher of the school was replaced by Saddam Hussein wife he was the deputy of the Iraqi president at that time, when she took over she transformed the school significantly, additional building was build with more classes, another building for arts activities and music and the court yard was expanded for children to play and saluting the Iraqi flag weekly ceremony. There were also buses to take the children from the school to their homes and vice versa if the parents pay some money to the school monthly. The school was organised and clean all the time, every Thursday all the pupils get out of their classes to salute the Iraqi flag ceremony and read the national anthem and if there were talented pupils who had high scores in the lessons they get rewarded, then all the pupils walk in a military march where the teachers give them military orders during the march then they dispersed and back to their classes, Saddam wife was always present in this ceremony and sometimes gives the military orders. Shawkey used to hear different female teachers speak about Saddam wife with jealousy, because she keeps on changing her boots every day and wearing expensive clothes, she liked to show off, but they were afraid from her. Sometimes Shawkey play with Saddam sons UDAY or QUSAY , both were in the school, Shawkey used to carry Uday or Qusay on his shoulder and walk with them, but Uday was aggressive he always kicks Shawkey when he carries him on his shoulder or punch him in the stomach because Shawkey was fat, this was enough for Shawkey to stop playing with him and play only with Qusay, once Saddame wife was standing at the entrance of the school gate and saw Shawkey playing with Qusay she told Shawkey while she was laughing (you are just a round ball), Shawkey laughed too. The first love in Shawkey's life was in that school, there was a girl her name was (WARKA'A) she go to the school with her sister in the same bus that Shawkey takes, she was white, has long black hair, black eyes and a bit taller than Shawkey , Shawkey used to look at her with admiration and trying to be close to her, but he did not know how to get her attention, in one time while it was break in the school front yard and all the students were playing there, Shawkey decided to play with Warka'a and get her attention, so he went and filled his mouth with water then stood in front of Warka'a, then he throw the full water in force on Warka'a face and clothes, she exploded in tears and went inside the school building to talk to a female teacher, the teacher came and started shouting at Shawkey for his bad behaviour, Shawkey told her that he did not want to hurt Warka'a or upset her , he just wanted to play with her, all that was not of use and his love died in his first try, Warka'a became avoiding him and did not talk with him ever. When Shawkey became nine years old his brother (AHMED) was born and

Shawkey's family became consist of his parents Karem and Samera, his sister Sama who were two years younger than him and his brother Ahmed who was nine years younger than him. Shawkey was white, had black hair, brown eyes and fat, his sister was brown, had black long hair, brown eyes , and slim, Ahmed was brown, had black short hair, brown eyes, and slim.

Teenage Period

Chapter 1

When Shawkey finished his primary school it was (1973) he was twelve years old, his parents enrolled him in (ALGARBIA) which means (western) intermediate school, it was also a well know school in Baghdad for its good education, in this school Shawkey found another hobby and that was table tennis, there were three table tennis in the back yard of the school, at the beginning he was amateur in the game but through time he loved the game and his skills improved, in the same period Shawkey's parents moved to a different house in a different area, Samera's mother owned a (600) metre square piece of land in an area called (JAMELA), it was an area where the people lived there were of higher level of education and income than ALTOBCHY, Samera's mother had also some money she gave it to Samera, this money and the money that Samera was saving, she started building the new house. The house consisted of a room for guest, three bedrooms one for Shawkey's parents, one for him and the third one for Sama and Ahmed, there was a kitchen, bathroom and a front and rear garden. After finishing the house Shawkey's family moved in, Karem sold the house in ALTOBCHY and bought a Moscovich car for the family transportation, Shawkey's house neighbour from the right was called (ABO LO'AY) they had four children the oldest called (LO'AY) he was a boy one year younger than Shawkey and they became friends, in front of Shawkey's house there was a house called (ABO ADEL) they had seven children and the father was a mechanic , the oldest child was a female, but still they call the father with the name of his oldest son (ADEL) there was another house across the street on the left of Shawkey's house they was called (ABO NAGLA'A) they had two teenage girls the oldest called (NAGLA'A). the area streets were not tarmac at the beginning, during winter the roads become slippery and you can stuck in the mud, however there was another resident who became famous because he had never stuck his orange Moscovich car in the mud, this situation continued until the council put sewers in the area and the roads were tarmac. In this house Shawkey bought a small table and made it as table tennis to play with his friend Lo'ay or one of his relatives when they visit him and slowly he became professional in the game and started winning his friends at school. In this school there was a math teacher known for his cruelty and disgust, he had a long, thick ruler he use it for punishing the students, if any student did not make his home work he would call the student in front of the class and asks him to open his hand, then he hit it strongly with the ruler which made the hand red and painful, therefore when he calls a name that student freeze to death, also that teacher was not polite he used to call the students who fell to give the correct answer to his question, he tells them (are you on drugs) or (are you a donkey), he also used to throw big filthy spits from his mouth at the back of his podium, his lesson was ugly and frightening, that was why all students used to do their home work.

After Shawkey finished his three years at the intermediate school, he was enrolled in (ALMARKAZIA) which means (central) secondary school, it is also a good school in Baghdad, he needed to study three years in this school to finish his secondary education like high schools in the west and get his baccalaureate exam which will decide his future and what college he will be enrolled in. At ALMARKAZIA Shawkey met his two friends (AUSAB and HAYTHAM) both were living in the same area where he was living with a bit distance between them. Shawkey used to visit them at their homes besides meeting them at school and they used to sit and discuss their study and life matters. During this period the BA'ATH party was in power, although the revenue of the Iraqi oil there were crisis happening like shortage of eggs or meat and you find long queues of people waiting to get their share, the disconnect of electricity for three to four hours a day, because there were not enough power stations to produce electricity, the people used to tell themselves that these crisis the government creates to keep the people busy away from politics, but no one dared to say that publically, because they knew that the whole family will be punished severely. Then the murders of what was called (ABO TOBER) which means (the father of cleaver) it was just an expression to express the actions of this killer, each week or so a family gets butchered by this maniac where all the member of the family cut with a cleaver while sleeping at night including children, he cuts their bodies to pieces, this created a horror in the public for several weeks and they started avoiding going out at night and locking their home doors. After several weeks the Iraqi television showed a man who supposedly to be ABO TOBER, the producer said that this man was wanted by the Interpol and no one was able to capture him in all Europe except the Iraqi police, the people at last got relaxed that this criminal was captured, but really was he a true maniac who likes to butcher his victims or he was one of the government scum to terrify the people and keep them busy, no one knows. In spite of the friendship between Shawkey and his neighbour Lo'ay there were problems occur between them sometimes, in one occasion there was an argument between them which led for Shawkey to push Lo'ay to the ground (Shawkey was bigger and taller than Lo'ay), Lo'ay hated Shawkey and decided to get revenge, in another day Shawkey was alone at home and while he was standing in the garden, Lo'ay spoke with him from behind the fence that separate the two houses and started provoking him, Shawkey replied in the same manner, at that time someone else appeared from the fence and that was one of Lo'ay relatives who was older than Shawkey, then both Lo'ay and his relative crossed over the brick fence and attacked Shawkey, because they were two they managed to put Shawkey to the ground and put his head in the garden soil, then they crossed the fence running away. When Shawkey's parents came back home from work, Shawkey told his mother of what happened, she was angry and went to ABO LO'AY house and complained to Lo'ay parents about this cowardice behaviour two against one, Lo'ay father apologised to Samera about the incident and told her that this will not happen again. When Samera went back home she told Shawkey that he must take lessons in self defence to defend himself, at that moment Shawkey remembered that his friend Musab was training in KARATE with a tutor who was his friend, so Shawkey decided to ask Musab to train with him. The tutor name was (FIRHAD) they use to train in different places like Firhad's home or Musab's home, but mostly in open parks, where they sit and Firhad starts teaching them the movements first before they start using it against each other to practice, he also taught them the KATA which was the pattern of fighting movements shows the student level in the KARATE training and learning. After learning Karate Shawkey regain his self confidence and knew that he can defend himself if he have to, because he knew how to punch and kick and when to direct his attack, but through time Shawkey forgot about his fight with Lo'ay and they became friends again and even Shawkey started teaching Lo'ay Karate in his own garden. When Shawkey started learning Karate he decided also to lose weight, so he went on strict diet, he used to take his breakfast, in the afternoon he takes only (4-5) biscuits and in the evening he takes (4-5) biscuits again, that was his all food plus some fruits, he used to feel very hungry, but did not give up he was determent to lose weight and becomes slim. After two months of this diet Shawkey lose significant weight and was happy with that.

At this period of Shawkey's life his new hoppy of corresponding was born, Shawkey use to see foreign movies on Iraqi television about the west , how they live their lives happily, sees the blonde females which was rare in Iraq, all this created a strong will for him to leave Iraq and live in the west, of course these films do not show the hardship in the western world, how people struggle to pay their taxes, hard to get jobs and keep it, but only show people laughing and enjoying their lives. At this period Shawkey was (16-17) years old, his hormones were on its peak, he decided to correspond with girls from the west, he started looking in newspapers and magazines about penpals , he found girls and boys from different countries, England, Australia, Indonesia, New Zealand, even he started corresponding with friends from Arabic countries like Egypt and Morocco, through time Shawkey found himself with (30-40) letters need to be answered, he started feeling bored from repeating writing these letters and stopped replying to all of them, except one female from Edinburgh in Scotland, because she kept on writing to him even when he do not answer her, which made him stick to her, her name was (Dona), she was a white girl, has black long hair, blue eyes , slim and (170) cm tall, she use to work in a restaurant in Edinburgh. Shawkey kept on corresponding with Dona, he even thought of inviting her to visit him in Iraq, when he told Samera about it his mother told him (where she will sleep, if she sleep in your bedroom, when then you will sleep) then she said (how you will spend on her, you are still a student and take your expenses from us and it is not enough to look after her, what the other people and your relatives will say about a foreign female lives with us), after her lecture Shawkey knew that the idea of inviting Dona to his home was impossible, he did not open the subject again with his mother and did not tell Dona about his idea.

During the summer holidays for the last two years of his secondary school, Shawkey found a job in one of the plastic factories that one of Lo'ay's relatives own, he wanted to collect some money, so he worked night shifts, through these six months holidays he managed to collect (600) Iraqi Dinars and he did not know what to do with it, Samera suggested that he can use it to travel and study in England, where there is a friend and relative to his father Karem living there his name was (MAHMOOD), he was a wealthy man and could look after Shawkey over there, Karem sent a letter to Mahmood and told him about the idea of Shawkey studying in England and how much the cost of education will be there, Mahmood contacted Kings college in London and gave them the information about Shawkey, then the college sent a letter to Shawkey in Iraq contained all the information about the facilities available, studying subjects and cost, the cost per year was £3000 pounds and of course this amount of money was too big for what Shawkey owned, at the same time the financial situation for Shawkey's parents was medium, they were not rich to afford this much money to spend on education per year, therefore the idea of studying in England was not possible. Shawkey was not bothered about it, because he was thinking that studying in Iraq was easier because it is all in Arabic not like England in English. Shawkey managed to get (82%) in his baccalaureate exam and he was accepted in the University of Technology in Baghdad to study Metallurgy and production engineering. Shawkey decided to buy a computer for him to help him in his study, he told Dona about his decision to continue studying in Iraq and his decision to buy a computer instead of travelling to England, after that Shawkey continued with his corresponding with Dona even after some months of starting his college until she sent him a letter telling him that she was engaged and will not be able to continue corresponding with him, Shawkey wished for her good luck and the corresponding stopped. About the computer which Shawkey bought it was in Basic language, he did not need it in his study, after all the troubles he faced from the security force in Baghdad to get permission to buy it, because in Iraq no one can buy a computer, printer, camcorder or any printing device without permission from the security force in case it would be used for political purposes, so he decided to sell it and buy a video cassette player to watch blue movies if he can get one!!!.

Chapter 1

When Shawkey joined the University of Technology to study his first degree in Engineering, Iraq was passing in a political turbulence, Shawkey was admiring Saddam Hussein character, his speeches attract every one listening to him and the youth would say that he was a revolutionary man aiming to achieve glory to Iraq and its people, Shawkey use to listen to him and get energised, while his father Karem always use to say that he is another agent for the American and do what he was told to do, Shawkey was not impressed with Karem ideas and rejecting it completely, In (1979) Saddam took the power in Iraq from the current president at that time Ahmed Al-Bakr who was his relative, and became the president of Iraq, people says that Saddam had forced Al-Bkre to resign after he made a conspiracy and killed the oldest son of Al-Bakr by what was look like a car accident and because Al-Bakr was afraid that more of his family will be killed, he resigned. After Saddam became the president, he immediately made a meeting for the Ba'ath party and executed sixteen of his fellow comrades in the party for treason, according to the Ba'ath party story that those traitors made a plan with the Syrian Ba'ath party and the president of Syria, who was at that time Hafiz Al-Asad, to make a coup and put someone sympathises with Hafiz Al-Asad, but the people say that Saddam killed his comrades because they rejected him to take over the power, he executed them as a punishment and lesson for others not to disagree with him in the future. When Al-Bakr was president of Iraq, on the east of Iraq its neighbour Iran was governed by the Shah, he was an alliance of the west and made Iran the fifth military power in the world, he always wanted to expand his border with Iraq to the benefit of Iran, there was Shat Al-Arab which is a river in the south of Iraq it's both sides belongs to Iraq, but the Shah wanted to expand Iran borders and take half of it and make the border pass in the middle of the river, Shat Al-Arab was a wide river and the only exit for Iraq to the Persian Gulf, through it Iraq use to make all its trades to the Gulf countries and the world, because the Ba'ath party at that time had recently took the power in Iraq at (1968) it was still military weak and have a small army, so the Shah started making provocations on the borders with Iraq by shelling the border cities and his army moves across the borders to occupy some of the cities for certain time before withdraw, the Iraqi side was not responding, because they know if it went to full scale war Iraq will lose and maybe there will be no more Iraq, so Saddam was the deputy of the president Al-Bakr and made a deal with the Shah called (Algerian treaty) in (1975), in that treaty Iran took half of the river Shat Al-Arab, in other term of the treaty Iraq should get rid of all oppositions of the Shah who lives in Iraq specially Khomeini, who was living in Najaf which is a holly city in the south of Iraq, in return all military provocations on the border seize and have permanent peace. Khomeini was kicked out of Iraq and went to France, so when he took the power in Iran and created the Islamic republic of Iran, he saw his enemy Saddam had took the power in Iraq, so he decided to get rid of Saddam and all the Ba'ath party government and make a new Islamic revolutionary state belong to Iran in Iraq.

Iraq demography of its population is complicated, majority of population are Arabic muslin Shi'a (70%) like all Iranian they are Iranian Muslim Shi'a, the other (30%) of the population in Iraq mostly are Arabic Muslim Sunni and other ethnic groups like Kurdish Muslim Sunni and Christians, the loyalty in Iraq is mainly to the tribe that they belong to, Saddam was Sunni, so he brought to the government many people from his town of birth Tikret and most of the important positions in the government or the army were given to the Sunni, only unimportant positions or small ranks were given to the Shi'a in order to control the Shi'a majority in Iraq, so in order for Khomeini to topple Saddam government he needs a Shi'a party to succeed with that, so he started to support Al-dawa party which was a Shi'a Islamic party, this party was cracked down by the Ba'ath government before and many of its members were arrested, however Khomeini started supporting the party financially to make new members and expand its base from the Shi'a in Iraq, Iran started sending them instructions on how making bombs and killing the members of the Ba'ath party, matters were getting intense between the two governments, then one day when Saddam was still deputy there was a meeting in the University of Al-mustansiriya for the students who are members in the Ba'ath party and one of the ministers in the government was present, the meeting was a celebration of the anniversary of the Ba'ath Coup in (1968) where the Ba'ath party took the power in Iraq, suddenly during the meeting one of the student started shouting anti government slogans then throw two hand grenades on the students, many of them were injured, but the minister was not, after the incident the investigation showed that the student was a member of Al-dawa party, then after three days, Saddam went there to the same locations and said clearly(I swear by God , I swear by God, I swear by God, that the blood spilt in Al-mustansiriya ground will not go in vain), there were hysteria slogans and calls for revenge. Then another savage crack down on Al-dawa party started, they were tortured and killed like animals. This all was happening in (1979) when Khomeini took the power in Iran, then when Saddam took the power in the same year, he decided it was time for revenge and that how the Iraq - Iran war started. The crack down on Al-dawa party continued, all the Iraqi Shi'a from Iranian origin or have Iranian roots were taken by lorries to the borders with Iran with nothing on them except their clothes, all their properties were taken by the government and given to regime supporters, those families that were arrested were insulted, beaten and raped by the security forces before taking them to the borders, all these actions infuriated Khomeini and the Iranian public, there were slogans in Iranian news papers and Iranian radio to get rid of Saddam and the Ba'ath government for all the atrocities that they were committing against the Shi'a in Iraq. Then Iran closed the borders with Iraq and shelling started from time to time from the Iranian side of the border to the Iraqi border cities, while that was happening Saddam started making several meeting with his military commanders to assess the Iraqi military situation, Iraq at that time was military strong and has a strong army, while Iran was relatively military weak, Khomeini had executed many experience military generals when he took the power, because they supported the Shah regime and Iran was still building its strength after cutting its relations with west and got out of the Nato alliance, so things was looking easy for Saddam to lunch a pre-emptive strike on Iran by occupying its border cities to put pressure on Khomeini and the Iranian government to stop supporting the Shi'a to overcome Saddam regime, that was what he was told. In (1980) Iraqi forces crossed the border with Iran and started occupying the Iranian border cities across the whole borders which is about (1000) kilometres with Iran from north to south, the Iraq – Iran war started and will last for eight years where both parties will lose one million dead from both sides, all this will happen because of two stubborn leaders who have personal vendetta.

Shawkey joined the University just before the war started in September (1979), it was a new build University teaching different engineering subjects, it was a new world for Shawkey, for the first time studying was mixed between males and females, before that they were separated in different schools, in this University he met his new friends (Shaker and Abdulla) in the college of Metallurgy and production engineering where he was studying, he spent the four years college with them, studying together and discussing their lives problems. Shawkey always considered that his study was more important than any other thing, so he kept on listening attentively to his tutors and write all their explanations and comments in his notebooks, so that he do not forget them when he study at home or revising for exams, because of that he attracted the attention of other students in his class and they started borrow his notebooks to read his notes and ask him about the ambiguous or unclear matters to explain it to them, part of these students was two girls (Su'ad and Nedwa), Su'ad was brown, has black long hair, brown eyes, Muslim, slim and (155)cm tall, Nedwa was white, Christian, has brown eyes, black long hair, slim and (150) cm tall, Su'ad use to laugh for any reason even a stupid joke, while Nedwa was more mature, Su'ad had attracted Shawkey's attention, he was still in his teenage years and this kind of female behaviour make him happy specially when laughing on his jokes, funny and stupid ones which made him attracted to her regardless of all the heavy makeup she use to put on her face, so the five of them Shawkey, Shaker, Abdulla, Su'ad and Nedwa became sitting together in the class room or the cafeteria and study together. Shawkey had strong personality, he likes to control other people, his ideas has to be implicated and adhered to , Shaker use to follow Shawkey's ideas without objection, but Abdulla had a strong personality too, he objects sometimes, when that happen Shawkey tolerate such objections to avoid a total disobedience. After the first year finished and starting the second year the was still in its early years, the government gave instructions to the Universities that during the summer holiday the students must serve in the public army which was a militia army build mostly from members of the Ba'ath party members and some other civilians who are not member in the party, their job was to guard the Universities and colleges in the evening and nights during the summer holiday and some of them were taken to guard another military posts in the north of Iraq where there was not enough army to guard them from the attacks of the Kurdish army called (Peshmerga), this Kurdish militia was employed by the Iranian to weaken Saddam army, when the summer holiday arrived Shawkey was called to serve in the University public army with other colleagues from his class and other classes, he attended the University and was introduced to his unit which consisted from colleagues from his class, he was given public military uniform and a Kalashnikov (AK-47) and ten bullets, then they were told to return on a different day to be transported to the north of Iraq, they were not told where. On the specific day he attended the University, there were big buses waiting for them and was told that they will be taken to Zakho, which was a town in the north of Iraq near the Turkish border, they will be responsible to guard a military post there, and then they were taken to the north. They arrived at night and were distributed each unit will guard a post, there were many posts each one called (Rebia) which was a structure build from mud on a high or relatively high hill to observe and control its surrounding area usually a valley, Shawkey Rebia was about fifty metres from the main road that take them to the main town of Zakho, this was from the back of the Rebia, all other sides of the Rebia except the front one were level ground with the main road, there were many trees on the right side of the Rebia, the front of the Rebia which was the side that they needed to monitor was descending in (30) degrees to an open wide valley, that continues several kilometres further down in a level ground until reaches the high mountains of the Turkish border, most of these Rabias were guarded by the public army some of these armies are consists of students from different colleges and Universities and some of them were from the areas in Baghdad, where each area has its own public army consists from the residents of that area, some of them were members of the Ba'ath party and others were not, no one can object or face the consequences, Shawkey's Rabia consisted of two low roof spaces to store the food supplies, one separate mud structure with roof and enough height as a kitchen, there were five metal camping beds to sleep five people, the distance between each Rabia and the other was (1-2) kilometres horizontally, when Shawkey's unit arrived they were told to avoid going to Zakho in the evening just in case there would be Kurdish militia there and they kill them, at night everyone must be on their Rabia to guard it, the reason for these instruction because in the last week one of the Rabias was attacked by the Kurdish and they chopped the heads of all the occupants of that Rebia, so they were on alert. Although these instructions, some members of the units use to go shopping for food, cigarettes (Shawkey was not a smoker at that time) or other items some times in the day time, but in groups of (2-3) people, the food supply for the Rabia comes once a week and should last for a week, but that was not the case sometimes the food finish and the students go shopping in Zakho, the water supply also weekly also, but on a different day, the food that was provided was rice, biscuits, cans of food, oil, salt and some meat, these supplies help to cook meals on a daily basis and each student has to cook in a certain day. There were cooking facilities like pans, plates, spoons, forks and knives and three small chairs. During Shawkey staying in the Rabia they did not face any attack, however other incidents occurred, once a scorpion appeared on the wall of the Rabia, it was dark yellow and small, Shawkey had never seen one before, panic station occurred, one said let us shoot it, another said (get away from it, it will jump on you), another said (hit it with the shovel), at the end one of the student hit it with the AK-47 bottom more than once then squashed it with his boot and panic station was over, then they were looking at each other and laughing, one of them said (this was only a miserable small scorpion what would you do if there was a Kurdish attack). After that seeing wild life became normal, in another time a snake was found in one of the small gaps in the Rabia, but it run away after it was frightened by the panic of the brave soldiers in the Rabia, in another time Shawkey saw a black water snake in one of the water channels there while he was pissing, his piss stopped automatically in the middle and he stepped back in a hurry two metres until the damn snake passed away. What was funny really the story of the eagle, once Shawkey saw an eagle flying over the Rabia, he kept on following its fight until the eagle stood on a branch of a high tree about fifty metres from him, Shawkey decided to hunt it, he carried his AK-47 and went walking slowly between the trees, then about ten metres from the eagle, he sat on his feet and aimed at the eagle, then pulled the trigger, the bullet went out, but from the reaction of the rifle he was pushed to the back and fall on his bottom, mean while the sound had frightened the eagle and started hovering over Shawkey's position, Shawkey was scared that the eagle will attack him, the manoeuvre of the eagle kicked the shit out of him, he was frozen and sweating, but thank God the eagle changed his mind and felt sorry for Shawkey and decided to fly away, there is no word can explains the relief that Shawkey felt at that time, so he decided to shut the fuck up and go back to the Rabia, when he got there, he tried to be as normal as possible and told his brave colleagues (like him) that he missed the eagle this time, may be next time, but in his own mind said (no way hosay). In another incident one of Shawkey's colleagues found a lost sheep, it was standing by itself on the front of the Rabia, there were no other sheep beside it or a Sheppard, particularly that week the starving soldiers had finished their weekly food supply in two days, so they were thinking of visiting Zakho, but here we go a miracle from God a lost sheep (or that what was decided), there was no disagreement what so ever about the fate of the poor sheep, the decision was made, cook it for lunch, one of the student was a son of a butcher, so he took the task of prepare it and another one will cook it, the process took about two and half hours to make it ready to eat, but eating it took only half an hour, yes a whole sheep was eaten in one meal by five people, then they started drinking tea and relaxed, suddenly a Sheppard appear, he was a small boy asking them if they saw a lost sheep, they were taken by surprise, however while they were looking at each other face one of them asked another one (did you see a lost sheep), the other was nodding by his head with answer (no) and the same question kept on repeating from one to another with serious faces, but no one had seen a lost sheep, so they told the Sheppard that they will let him know if they see one, the poor boy smiled, saluted them and walked away, at that time they were smiling to each other with naughty look, but no one said anything.

After finishing the service of the public army at the end of the summer holiday which lasted for three months, they were returned to the University to give back their military uniforms and their weapons.

Since Shawkey joined the University, the Ba'ath party members in his college tried more than once to make him join the party, but Shawkey always used to answer them politely that he support the government in all its programmes, but he prefers to be independent. During the Iraq – Iran war his mother Samera was very angry on Saddam and his Ba'ath party government particularly on Saddam for starting a war with Iran, she was despise them when they show on the TV the dead bodies of the Iranian soldiers and committing on that by saying (these are the rotten bodied of the Persian, fire worshipper, to hell with them and that what they deserve), that was painful showing dead bodies, cursing them and calling them fire worshipper like their ancient ancestors who used to do that, they are Shi'a and Muslim now not fire worshippers, and she used to say that this war was unjust, while his father Karem he always was cursing Saddam and his regime, besides all of that the Imam of the Shi'a in Iraq his name (Mohammed Baqir al-hakem) was living in Iran as opposition to Saddam and all the Shi'a support him, he was from the same family that Shawkey belongs to, but from different branch he was from the Najaf branch, but Shawkey was from Baghdad branch, regardless of that the suspicious of the Ba'ath party members to Shawkey and his family was always there and remarks always said about the difference between the two branches of Al-hakem family, so Shawkey was not willing to join the Ba'ath party, however he heard from his colleagues in the college including Shaker and Abdulla that who wants to continue his study for the master degree must be a member of the Ba'ath party, so Shawkey started discuss this matter with his parents and express his wish to continue his study for the master degree, at the end they agreed for him to join the Ba'ath party. After several days a member of the party in his class spoke with Shawkey about joining the Ba'ath party, Shawkey agreed, this student took Shawkey to an empty room in one of the building in the University and gave him a joining form, it was written on it a declaration that the person who join the party must declare his membership whenever asked and if he do not he will be executed, he must a true believer with the principals of the party and the leadership of Saddam Hussein as the leader of the Ba'ath party, then Shawkey had to sign it and date it and became a member of this party to stop the Ba'ath party members following and harassing him, also a step forward to continue his master degree in the future. Shawkey's continued as usual except that each week he had to attend a party meeting which lasts usually for an hour , the meeting consists of one member of the party with a little higher rank than the rest of the people attending (they are more like audience than participants), sometimes this person who control the meeting invites a guest who was also of a high rank in the party rank sequence, the contents of the meeting , first starting with reading the names of the people who were present (Shawkey never attended a meeting without absence of other members and usually the present people were far less than the absentees) and most of the meeting time spent on criticise the absentees, so the present people were take the grieve that should be given to the absentees, this usually takes most of the meeting time, then what was left of the meeting time the controller starts talking and discussing the Ba'ath party principals (which were mostly common sense sentence does not need atomic physics to understand) or explaining one of Saddam sentences in one of his speeches (which was also another waste of time) and the controller keeping calling Saddam the hero, the struggling leader, the president, the engineer (from where he became engineer, he left education after finishing his secondary school) and so on. Sometimes the controller speaks about Iraq – Iran war and keeping calling the Iranian that they were fire worshippers not Muslims (big lie) and that America and Israel the enemies of the Arab and Saddam was the only one who stood against them and he was the true leader of the Arab nation, this nonsense repeated every meeting like a (donkey mill).

Shawkey's relationship with Su'ad was as a colleague, with time he was attracted to her, but in the third year at college she started walking with another student and sit with him separately, Shawkey became annoyed , then she went absent for two weeks from the college, when she came back she told Shawkey, Nadwa and the rest of the gang that she was engaged to one of her relatives, this news made Shawkey sad, but he did not show that to his friends, he was suffering that inside him and at home, even sometimes he cried at home, because he lost her, he knew that if he tells his mother about her and that he want to marry her, Samera will refuse that and tells him that he was still a student and he has a long way in his life to study. After the third year had finished and the fourth year started, which was the last year in the college, Shawkey found himself that his attraction to Su'ad had disappeared, he started getting closer to Nedwa the Christian, in one time he was sitting with her alone and tried to know more about her, because she was Christian he wanted to know her culture and family traditions about marriages between Muslims and Christians, he asked her a general question, but of course as a female she got the hint, she told him that Christians in Iraq they only marry people from the same religion and if a girl married a Muslim, she will be thrown out of the family and disowned her, she would not find any one to support her, all this to prevent Christians from changing their religion, Shawkey knew that he cannot marry Nedwa or any Christian female, because of their traditions. Then the final exams at the end of the year came, Shawkey became very busy revising for the exams, he studied heavily, because he wanted to get high marks, so that he can continue his study for the master degree. When the results of the exams came Shawkey found that he got good marks in the subjects (70%), but he scored higher marks in his final year project and got (80%), so the average score was (75%), this mark was the second in the level of marks in his college, he was the second student in the Metallurgy and production engineering to get this mark from the forty students in his class. Shawkey was very happy, because he knew that he can continue his study for the master degree.

Shawkey finished his college and got his bachelor degree in Metallurgy and production engineering, at that time the Iraq – Iran was in its fifth year, he was called to the army to serve his mandatory military service as a graduate which suppose to last for two years, he was sent to ABU GHRAIB military camp for check up and make a decision to elect him to be a soldier or an officer in the army, Shawkey past all the checks, but when the time came to make a decision of his status in the army he was sent to a room where there were three high rank officers, they knew he was from Al-hakem family, one of them was sarcastic when asked the question (which Al-hakem family you belongs to, Najaf or Baghdad), Shawkey replied (Baghdad), any way it was waste of time, because they had already made up their minds to make him a soldier, this was part of the discrimination that Saddam used to discriminate between the Shi'a and the Sunni in Iraq, they were Sunni officers. After that he was sent to Hilla (which was a city in the south of Iraq about 50 kilometres from Baghdad) military camp, to train him on using AK-47, military march and other rules, the period would be three months. There were no incidents during the training period, then he was sent to Taji military camp in Baghdad to spend the rest of his military service. Shawkey's unit was about twenty Soldiers most of them engineers, some of them from his own class mates and others from other engineering colleges and few non graduate soldiers, the officers accompanied the unit were engineers from other colleges, the regime wanted to allocate graduate students in non fighting locations like factories, so they get use of their knowledge, therefore Shawkey's unit was allocated at an armour factory to repair tanks and armour vehicles, it was build within a small military camp in the middle of the huge Taji military camp. Shawkey's camp was led by a colonel called (Al-affas) he was an engineer and Sunni from Mosul city in the north of Iraq, his tribe known of their obedient to Saddam and many of them were in the army, they follow the army rules strictly, when the graduates arrived they were divided into small units, each unit was consist of twenty soldiers (all of them engineers) and one officer who was an engineer, too. The work in the camp starts with the morning inspection of the soldiers for the cleanness and tidiness of their uniform, boots, hair and nails, then the morning exercises start consisted of running in a circle, other exercises to arms and legs, after that the soldiers march to the factory to do their tasks for the day. They work until one o'clock then they get lunch where food was cooked for them and they eat it, at two o'clock they go back to the factory to continue their tasks for that day, they finish at (3.30 pm), they gather in the exercise open ground to call them by name and make sure everyone was present, then at (4.0 pm) Al-affas leaves the camp and follow him the other officers and then the soldiers (usually the soldiers carried by open lorries), there was a system if someone lives in Baghdad they can go back home for the rest of the day and come back to the camp early in the next morning, but if the soldier lives outside Baghdad he gets a room in a caravan with other soldiers who have a situation like his to sleep in it for a month and at the end of the month they get a week holiday to go and see their families. Besides the usual duties in the factory there were guarding duties for the rest of the day, where were certain positions of the camp needed to be guarded in the evening and night by soldiers usually (3-4) depending on the location that they guard and this appeared on a daily basis on the duties sheet that was hanged outside the duties office, each soldier has weekly duty where he spend his evening and night at the camp either once or twice a week depending on the soldiers availability in the camp like in some cases where there were too many soldiers on holiday the present soldiers in the camp do more night duties, that was very annoying because they had enough of the military rules in the day and want to get some good sleep and rest at home, the duties start from (4.30 pm) till (6.0 am) where they give back their weapons and prepare themselves for the morning inspection at (7.30 am). The punishment system in the camp was if someone had a long hair or long beard during the inspection process , he would be put on duty that day (means he will spend his night in the camp), if someone comes late in the morning to the camp he will be put on duty that day, if someone was not present at (3.30 pm) for the countdown, means he escaped from the camp during the day to go back home, he would put in prison after shaving his whole head which was a shame, also at night the soldiers divide the night hours between them where one soldiers stay awake to guard his post, weapon and his colleagues weapons, if he fall to sleep, there were some evil officers at night they make inspections to the posts and if they see a soldier sleeping on his turn, they take his weapon or his colleagues weapons (they are sleeping of course) and give it to the duty office in the morning, which will inform Al-affas about it and that soldier will be head shaved and put in the prison for some days. Because of all of that soldiers use to stick to the rules specially the engineers. The kind of tasks the engineers use to do in the factory like making bolts or gears for the vehicles using milling machines, making engineering drawings for parts need to be either make or imported for the tanks or armour vehicles.

This period of Shawkey's life was boring hateful and there was no improvement only military rules and orders, but in the same time shaped and polished his personality it changed him from a boy to a man who understand the meaning of responsibility and wise thinking, however it made him learn a new bad habit and that was smoking, boredom on long night duties make soldiers look for some kind of enjoyment, for Shawkey it was smoking. At the beginning it was like a game felling the numbness when he smoked his first cigarettes, in time he became addicted to it, in many times when Shawkey was doing his night duties, he use to look to the sky and stars and thinks if there was someone looking at him from the other star at the same time, he was feeling miserable and kept on repeating a question he leaned when he was at the first class of his primary school and that was (till when the camel stays on the hill), the answer was (till dusk), Shawkey used to repeat this sentences and wondering when his military service will finish. One incident occurred during this period, one day he awoke late in the morning, he knew if he was late he will spend his night on duty at the camp, he left home like a crazy to get to the camp as quick as possible, he knew that the inspection time was (7.30 am) and the time was (6.30 am) it would be a miracle to get in time to the camp, he got a transportation to Taji camp, then he used hitchhiking method to get to his camp, he got to the outside metal mesh fence, now how the hell he will get inside, the gates of the camp closes at (7.0 am) and now it was (7.15 am), plus he did not want any one from the camp to see him late and grassed him up to Al-affas who will put him on duty that day, so Shawkey started looking for a gap between the fence and the ground to crawl under it, and here we go he found enough gap to do that, he crawled under the fence and when he was about to stand up his outside military jacket caught up with one of the edges of the fence which caused a small tear in his jacket, but never mind he made it and now he was inside the camp, he put his jacket somewhere safe and went to the exercise ground to join his colleagues in his unit, these last minutes was the most critical minutes in his life, when he got home that evening he sewed the jacket and kept using it for many years to come until he arrived to England as later we will see. Shawkey's military service continued for three years instead of two years because of the Iraq – Iran war, in (1986) he received his acceptance in the University of Technology to continue his study for the master degree, his acceptance came in the same time of releasing him from the army, he was very happy he was civilian at last.

Chapter 1

The master study period in Shawkey's life was a new experience, many changes occurred, the first one was selling his parents house in (GAMELA) where he lived all the past period to another area which was a posh area in north of Baghdad called (AL-KAFA'AT) which means (post graduates), its people are mostly rich and of high level of education, his home consisted of two bedrooms, one for Shawkey and the other for his sister Sama and his brother Ahmed, there was a living room , one guest room and kitchen and a bathroom. There was medium size front garden and a small side garden on the left side of the house, there was a long garage and the whole house was build from solid concrete. On the left side of the house there was an empty piece of land then a house called (ABO EHSAN) they have six children the oldest was their daughter Ehsan, on the right there was a house called (ABO KALDON) only the husband and wife were living there and their only son Kaldon was living independently in SAMARA which was a city in the north of Iraq. In front of Shawkey's house there was a large empty land then a row of houses, the area was still new not many houses were build there at that time, Al-kafa'at was close to two areas one was called (KATHRA) and the other one called (AL-AMERIA), both areas are reasonably posh. There was a long road separate Al-Kafa'at from Al-ameria, on the right side of the road there was a large open space for horse training and on the left side there was row of houses which were the border of Kathra. Shawkey's father Karem had a relative lived in Kerbala, which was a holly city in the south of Iraq about one and half hour drive from Baghdad, his name was (JALEL) he have two girls and two boys the oldest son his name was Samy, Shawkey's parents visited Jalel from time to time and he did the same, once when Shawkey was visiting Jalel with his parents, Shawkey went for a walk in Karbala, in the way he saw a group of people were gathered near one of the shops and they were laughing, Shawkey walked through them to see what they were laughing at, he saw an adult man clearly suffering from mental health problems holding the end of a hose which was connected to a bicycle air pump, the air pump was with a man telling him to put it inside his arse hole, so that he push air inside it and he will become fat, the poor man with the mental health was putting the hose inside him and waiting to become fat, he was laughing like the rest of the crowd, but he did not know what he was doing, Shawkey smiled to the scene, but felt sorry for the man and he could not do something about it otherwise he will anger the crowd, so he left the scene.

When Shawkey started his master degree he met new friends in his class they were studying engineering management degree, one of them his name was (HAZEM) he was also in his class when he was studying his first degree, Hazem was the cause for Shawkey to lose his virginity as we will see. Shawkey was still virgin at that time although he was twenty five years old, he never believed that there was a friendship between boys and girls, if he sees a boy with a girl in the street close to each other he would think that they were either relatives, brother and sister, engaged or married couple, he would never believed that they were friends, because friendship was forbidden in the Iraqi society and the Arab world including Islam and if there was a friendship or relationship between them and the family of the girl knew about it they would kill the girl, all girls must be virgin when they get married, if the husband found that his pride was not virgin in their first night he would kill her, too. This is called honour killing and the killer does not get much sentence may be six months, if he got sentenced at all. After passing few months of Shawkey's study and his friendship with Hazem improved, once he was discussing the matter between boys and girls with him, Hazem was telling him how he goes to visit his girlfriend at night and sleep with her while her parents were sleeping, Shawkey was listening to him and at the end he told him that he did not believe him, because there was no thing as friendship between boys and girls, at that time Hazem told Shawkey (ok then my girlfriend will call you tonight), Shawkey told him (whatever) and left him he did not take his words seriously. That evening around eight o'clock his home phone rang, so Shawkey picked the other phone from his room, there was a girl on the other side asked to speak with Shawkey, he told her that he was, then she said (how are you and how is the family) Shawkey thought that she was one of his relatives, he replied (they are alright), then asked her (who are you) she replied (you did not know me) he said (no), then she said (alright I will go now, bye) and hanged up the phone. Shawkey was wondering who was that, if she was one of his relatives then why she did not spoke with his mother or father and she just hanged up the phone, while he was wondering the phone rang again, this time it was Hazem, he asked Shawkey if his girlfriend called him, Shawkey told him that no one called him except a girl asked him about himself and his family and their well being and she hanged up, he started laughing and told Shawkey (that was my girlfriend Warda), Shawkey lost speech, he was so surprised that a girl has the guts to call a strange boy to her and speak with him like that, then and only then he believed that there was friendship between girls and boys and it was not a myth. In the next day when he saw Hazem he told him how he was surprised by her phone call and asked him if Warda has a friend who would like to know Shawkey at least just for talking on the phone, although Shawkey was having other plans, Hazem told him that he will ask her. Three days past Shawkey asked Hazem if there were any developments, he told him not at the moment, then in the fourth day Hazem told Shawkey that Warda gave him her friend Zahra's phone and she want Shawkey to call her, because this was the first time ever Shawkey was about to speak with a strange girl to him, he was afraid he may speak with one of her family and what he will tell them, besides that he know himself that he was not a good liar he cannot make a lie on the spot and continue with it, he will put himself in an embarrassing situation, for all these reasons he told Hazem that it was better if Zahra make the first call, then he will call her later. That evening about eight o'clock Zahra called, Shawkey's mother Samera picked the phone in the living room and Zahra asked her to speak with Shawkey, Samera came and asked Shawkey in his room (there is a girl on the phone wants to speak with you, who she was) Shawkey told her (it was a girl he met her) Samera asked (and what she wants from you, you must be careful there are bad girls who want to trip the boys in their nets) Shawkey replied (do not worry she is just a friend, there is nothing between us and I am careful), then Shawkey lift the phone and waited until Samera hanged up the phone in the living room, then he said (hello) Zahra said (hello, Shawkey) he said (yes) she said(I am Zahra, how are you), he said and the sweat started moving on his forehead (good, and you) she said (good) then he said (how you got my phone) she said (Warda gave it to me and told me that you want to speak with me) he said (this is true, I feel bored and lonely and need to speak with a girl on the phone may be we become friends) she said (how friends) he said (means we talk with each other on the phone when we have the time to know each other better) she said (I do not mind and what is after that) he said (I would like our friendship to be open without conditions, if we find that we like each other, then we can go out together and have a nice time) she said (will this include sex), Shawkey thought for a moment what to say, he do not want her to run away, but he decided to tell her honestly what he wanted in a gentle friendly way so that he do not frighten her, he said(as I said I want our friendship to be open, if we like each other then we can have sex too, if we did not like each other then it will be friendship by phone) there was a quiet period Shawkey was worried from Zahra's answer, then she said (I do not mind) Shawkey was relieved and happy, because he knew that he was going the right way to satisfy his desires and have sex without ties, he always preferred to be honest and do not lie, because he do not want someone in the future tells him that he lied to him or her, he knows also that he will not open a girl and make her lose her virginity, because that will mean a death sentence for her and no one will marry her, also he cannot take that on his conscious. The phone call continued, he asked her about what food she liked, which colours she prefers, she asked him the same questions, after half an hour the phone call was ended after she told him that she will call him in the next day when she has the time. Shawkey met Hazem the next day and told him about the phone call, but he omitted the part concerning the sex, they were laughing and Hazem told him that he will be spoiled. That evening she called, Shawkey was waiting eagerly for her phone call, when the phone ranged he picked it up quickly before Samera does, Zahra said (I am calling you as promised) he said (I waited for your call eagerly and could not stop thinking about you all day, did you think about me) she said (yes I thought about you too, even at school), both Warda and Zahra were in the same secondary school in their area, Warda was seventeen years old and Zahra was eighteen years old, then Shawkey started asking her about her school and what she done, then started asking her naughty questions which were the type of questions that he liked, he said (what are you wearing) she said (red nightie) he asked (and what you wear under it) she said (bra and knickers) he asked (what colour is your bra) she said (white) he asked (and knickers) she said (white) Zahra was answering Shawkey's questions in a naughty way also, she knew Shawkey's intentions inside her and she liked it, then Shawkey asked (describe yourself to me from top to bottom) she said (I has black hair reaches my shoulders, brown eyes and slim) he asked (describe for me your breast , the size of your tits) she said (they are not big) he asked (is it orange size or lemon size or bigger) she laughed and said (I have not measured it, but they are same as orange size) he said (I like this size, I want to hold your tits with my hand) she laughed, then he asked (what is the colour of your nipples) she said (brown) he said (I want to suck these nipples) Zahra was laughing from Shawkey's questions, then he asked (describe to me your pussy, is it shaved or hairy) she said (shaved) he said (I like hairy pussy) she said (I always shave it for cleanness) he said (honestly I want to sleep with you, I am very anxious to see you and sleep with you) she said after a bit of quietness (I am also anxious to see you, but I do not know about sleeping with you, it is too early) he said (I am anxious to see you and you are the same, why delaying it, I want to eat you like a sandwich) she said (I know that) he said (then when we will meet) she said (at the end of the week on Thursday, there will be celebrations in the school and I will skip the school and meet you), the phone call was on Thursday, so there will be a whole week before their meeting, but Shawkey had no option but to accept, they agreed to meet in an area near to Zahra's school, where Shawkey will come in his father car (a pick up) to pick her up to his home at Al-kafa'at, Shawkey knows that his father leaves his car at home when he goes to work, so that Shawkey picks his mother when she finish her work at (4.30 pm) to bring her home and in the evening he goes to bring his father from the café where he meets his friends after work to bring him home, therefore the morning period between ten where the appointment was till he return Zahra back home at (2.30 pm) which was the time for her to finish school, was suitable for them to have enjoyable time together. In the next week an incident occurred caused Shawkey to know another girl who will make him very attached to her and love her, and that was incident (Aida).

On Sunday while Shawkey was in his room about (9.0 pm) waiting for Zahra phone call, the phone rang he picked it up quickly as usual, there was a female voice on the other side different from Zahra's voice, she said (hello), he said (hello) she said (I want to speak with Sa'ed), Shawkey politely said (I think it is a wrong number, there is no one here with name Sa'ed, bye), then Shawkey thought maybe it was a genuine mistake there was no reason to rush to conclusions, may be also she was a girl want to play with boys by phone, he waited to see what will happen, after three minutes the phone rang she was the same girl that ranged earlier, she said (is this the house of Sa'ed) he said (I think it is a wrong number, there is no one here with the name Sa'ed) she said (sorry) and hanged up, then Shawkey decided if she calls again he will play with her too, he waited for her to call eagerly, the next few minutes were the longest in his life and he forgot about Zahra's call, after three minutes the phone rang again and it was that girl, she said (I do not know why the phone ring on your end, the number I have must be for Sa'ed), Shawkey said in a naughty way politely (this number is mine, but there is no Sa'ed here, can I help you instead of Sa'ed) Shawkey was smiling waiting for her answer, she said (and who are you), he said (I am Shawkey , and I am engineer, who is Sa'ed) Shawkey knew that Sa'ed was not existed was just an excuse for her to call boys, she said (he is one of my relatives, he told me to call him) he said (what is your name, I want you to tell me your real name, I have told you my name) she said (Aida) he said (it is a nice name and his owner has a nice voice, too) she laughed and said (your voice nice too, where you live) he said (at Al-kafa'at, and you where you live) she said (your area is known a nice area, I live in Hai Al-amel, but we are thinking of moving from here because it is a common area) then Aida said (are you single or married) he said (single, bored and feeling lonely, and you are you single or married) she said (I am still a student in my secondary school, single of course, but why you feel bored and lonely) he said (because all I have in my life is my study, there is no girl to speak with or go out with her as a friend) she said (why you do not get married, you will has a wife to go out with her) he said (I am still studying there is no time for getting married, I personally do not want to get involved until I finish my study, and you do you have friends you speak with them), she said (I have friends in the school, but they are obnoxious), at that time Shawkey decided to get straight in the subject, he said (I am attracted to your voice and would like us to be friends, talk with each other when have the time to know each other better and who knows may be our friendship will develop) she said (how develop) he said (I like always to be honest, I like our friendship to be open with no promises or ties, we talk on the phone and may be go out if possible and see how things go on) she said (honestly, Sa'ed matter was a lie, I was sitting with my younger sister at home, my parents went out and we decided to make phone calls randomly for a laugh, but when I spoke with you I liked your voice and decided to call you again, I am a girl wearing Hijab not like other girls who play with boys) he said (I am sure you are polite, honest girl that is why I like your style of speaking in the phone and that is why I want us to be friends, maybe we like each other , but I do not like to give promises, what you say), after a short pause, she said (I do not mind being friends there is no harm from friendship, but there is no sex in our friendship) he said (do not say no and put conditions, I do not like conditions, leave the matter take its course and see what happen, do we have agreement) after another pause, she said (ok, I do not mind) he said (do you like to give me your phone number or you prefers that you call me) she said (I will not give you my phone number, because I do not know you, maybe I will give it to you in the future, I will be calling you) he said (I do not mind and you can call me any time in the evening , thank you for the call, nice meeting you) she said (nice meeting you too, bye) then she hanged up. Shawkey could not believe himself, he just had convinced a stranger girl to him by phone to be his friend, although he was not sure if she will call him again he still was happy with himself, at that moment Zahra called and said (I was trying to call you several times, the phone was always busy) he said (sorry, my mother was speaking on the phone with a relative) then Shawkey continued to talk with Zahra and agreed that both of them were waiting anxiously to meet and have some fun. Shawkey continued to think about Aida and her phone call, at the same time he was thinking of Thursday and the meeting with Zahra to sleep with her, in the evening next day Aida called Shawkey and he started to ask her his naughty questions to get her use to the matter, he asked (what you wear at home) she said (either a nightie or a pyjama) he said (is there a colour you prefer) she said (no I do not have any preferred colour, any colour will do) he said (what about your underwear) she said (what you mean) he said (the colour of your bra and knickers) she said (what kind of questions these are, is this part of our friendship) he said (it is just curiosity I like to know what colours you like, if you continue to stop me in every question then how we will know each other) she said (I did not mean that, I just was surprised with the kind of your questions) he said (there is no problem, now which colours you prefer) she said (I always prefer the bra white) he said (and colour of the knickers) she said (I knew that you will ask that, I prefer it to be white, but sometimes I wear red) he said (I like the red one) she said (why) he said (because it is more suitable for the girl) then he said (I like always to speak with a naughty girl, because she make me find words to speak with her and that make me horny) she said (and is this important) he said (of course important, because it makes me attached to the girl) all these were attempts to make Aida forget the shyness and become more open, then he asked (describe yourself to me) she said (I am just ordinary girl, I has a nose, one mouth, and two legs to walk) she was laughing, Shawkey laughed too and said (you know what I mean, your hair, eyes and so on) she said (I have black long hair when I remove the Hijab, brown eyes and I am white) he said (I like white girl) she said (that is good) he asked (describe for me your body) she said (I am slim, but have curves in the right places) he said (I like the girl with curves because it makes her more sexy, what is the size if your tits is it orange size or bigger) she laughed and said (what kind of a question is that, just a minute I will measure it, it is orange size or a bit bigger) she was laughing, Shawkey laughed too, and asked (and what is the situation with your pussy, is it shaved or hairy) she said (I knew that you will go down there, it is just a pussy like your God created it and hippy) they both were laughing, then Shawkey said (I like it hippy like a jungle) she said (why) he said (because it will has its sexy smell and if you sweat the smell become even sexier) she said (how you know that) he said (it is natural matter, every human being has his own smell and these parts have its smell too) she laughed and said (you are naughty boy and devil, you must know many girls) Shawkey said innocently (you are the first girl in my life and I do not have experience with any other girl, that is why I am asking you these questions to know) she said (I am also do not have experience and you are the first boy in my life), then Shawkey said (I am very anxious to see the owner of this nice voice and sense of humour) she said (me too, I am also want to see this devil boy with his naughty questions, but the matter still too early between us) she was laughing, Shawkey said (no problem I will wait until you have mercy on me and let me see you) she laughed and said (alright, I will go now and talk with you in another time) he said (alright have a nice night and sleep well, bye) she said (bye). Aida voice and conversation were very erotic to Shawkey which made his penis hard. After the phone call Shawkey continued to think about Aida and imagine how she looks like, she stuck in his head and Zahra did not call that evening.

On Tuesday no one called Shawkey, but on Wednesday Zahra called to ascertain the Thursday meeting, she said (we are on our appointment tomorrow) he said (of course, I am very anxious to see you and sleep with you, do not worry I will not put it completely inside your pussy , because I know that you are virgin, I do not want to open you, because we are friends and I do not want something wrong to happen to you) she said (I trust you) he asked (are you also anxious to sleep with me) she said (yes) he asked (so what you want me to do to you) she said (I do not know, do all what you want to do) he said (I will make you enjoy every minute of it) she said (I know that) then they talked normal conversation about her school and the phone call ended. When the phone hanged up it rang again and it was Aida, she said (your phone was busy) he said (my mother was talking on the phone) she said (how are you, I am sorry I could not call you yesterday my family were at home, I could not find a time to call) he said (I do not want you to put yourself in a difficult situation, call me when you feel safe to do that), then he asked (did you think about me, I have not stopped thinking about you and every time I remember your conversation and jokes my cock gets hard) she laughed and said (oh, wow, if my voice can do that then what will happen when you see me) he laughed and said (I do not know what I will do, but I know one thing and that I want to see you) she said (and what will happen if you did not like me, will you run away) he said (I do not think so, I know that I will like you from your beautiful voice) she said (I know that you will like me, I am white and curved in my bottom and thighs) he said (when I will see you then) there was a short pause then she said (may be next week , after my school finish at (1.30 pm) on Sunday, we have less lessons that day and we can meet at a suitable distance from my school and we go to a public park near my area to talk a bit, then you return me near my home because I do not want to be late and raise suspicions) he said (good idea, then I will see you on Sunday) she said (agreed, but I want to tell you from the beginning that there are a little remains of spots on my face) he said (and what is wrong with that, it is a normal process in all young people to have spots once in their lives, I myself had spots then it gone with growing up) she said (ok then, I agree to see you on Sunday) then she said (I cannot take long in the conversation because my parents will come back soon, I will call you in another time, bye) he said (bye) and the phone call ended. Shawkey was very happy because he made an appointment to see Aida next week.

Chapter 3

Shawkey's study in the University was in shape of lectures, some days he had many lectures from different lecturers and other days few lectures, his studying days not separated along the week Saturday to Thursday and Friday off day (Friday is the official Islamic holiday in the week in Islamic countries including Iraq), Saturday and Monday were long days for Shawkey, Sunday was short day and Tuesday, Wednesday and Thursday were off days for him to prepare the material required for his thesis, so he had enough time for his study and playing with girls, therefore his appointments with Zahra and Sunday with Aida were suitable for him, he was a handsome young man and engineer which make any girl wish to have him, he was sure of himself that Zahra and Aida will like him.

At last Thursday came, Shawkey took his father car and went to the meeting location at ten o'clock, after fifteen minutes two girls came in school uniforms, he knew Zahra from her description and clothes, she was carrying a small red hand bag, she was not beautiful like Shawkey thought, she was brown, had black long hair, slim and look older than eighteen years old, the other girl he knew later was Warda (Hazem's girlfriend), she was more attractive than Zahra and younger than her, she was brown, had black long hair, shorter than Zahra about (150) cm tall and also slimmer, Shawkey liked her more, but what can he do she was his friend girlfriend, so he said to himself (something better than nothing). Zahra left Warda and entered the Nissan pickup truck with Shawkey and drove towards his home at Al-kafa'at, both Shawkey and Zahra were reluctant to speak at the beginning, but with time they got comfortable and Shawkey started ask Zahra if she faced any problems in her way to see him, she told him that everything was alright. When they got to Shawkey's house, he took her to his bedroom and asked her if she likes to have tea or juice, she told him (no), the time was (11.15 am),because Zahra's area was one hour drive from his area with the traffic, after sitting for five minutes beside each other on the bed, Shawkey did not know what he should do, then Zahra said (I am here beside you, do what you want) he said (I will leave the room and you take off your clothes and get inside the bed, cover yourself and call me when you are ready) he left the room and closed the door, he waited for five minutes, when he did not heard her voice he knocked on the door and opened it, her clothes were on a chair and she was in bed covered, Shawkey sat on the bed and started taking off his clothes except his pants, then went inside the bed, he started kissing her mouth (he did not know how to kiss, but Zahra was better than him, then he took off his pants, removed the cover of the bed and sat on top of her, she was still wearing her bra and knickers, he helped her to remove the bra , he removed her knickers, her body was brown, slim, her tits were like lemons size and small nipples which proves that she had never had sex before or just few times, her pussy was small shaved . Shawkey started to kiss her from top to bottom, he kissed her mouth while he was squeezing her tits, then he started sucking her nipples, it was nice taste, at that time Zahra's eyes were open all the time which made Shawkey uncomfortable, he thought that she might not feeling comfortable or enjoying what he was doing, but she was smiling to him, after this foreplay he held his cock it was hard like iron and started rubbing it with her clits and pussy he started felling that her pussy became wet and she started closing and opening her eyes , he knew that she was enjoying what was happening, Shawkey continued to rub his cock with Zahra's wet clits until he was ready to come, he took tissues and came inside it, he did not want to come on her pussy to prevent the possibility of her getting pregnant, then he went to the bath room to wash his penis and came back to bed. Zahra was sleeping beside him and smiling to him, he smiled to her, but he did not feel that enjoyment that he was expecting, he did not know what was the problem, but he was not fully comfortable, Zahra asked (did you enjoyed that) he said (yes), she put her head on his chest . Both stayed in bed, Shawkey started to smoke a cigarette, then from the effect of Zahra's breasts and body touching his body, his cock became hard again, he asked Zahra (do you like us to do it again) she replied (as you like), this time he made Zahra take a doggy position to enter her from her bottom, when he started to push it in her arsehole, he was feeling a bit difficulty, it was very tight, so he started pushing it slowly inside then take it out, so that he do not hurt her, he continued with this process until his cock was inside her in a suitable distance, then he started push it in and out regularly in a uniform hits again and again till he reached his climax, then he rejected his seamen in tissues, the only thing that bothered him was that a bit of her feces was at the tip of his cock, after that he went to the bath room and washed his penis and came back to lay with Zahra in bed. Shawkey was satisfied with sex now, he asked Zahra if she wants tea, she accepted, then both of them wore their clothes and he made tea. At one o'clock it was a suitable time to take Zahra back home, she should be finishing school at (2.30 pm), he thanked Zahra for the nice time that they spent together and told her to call him in the evening as usual, then he took her to a place near her home, so that no one see them together and went back to his home to wait for his mother finishing time to go and pick her up from work. This was the first and the last time Shawkey saw Zahra, he did not felt the enjoyment that he was expecting, Zahra was not that beautiful and her area was too far from his, also after knowing Aida that was enough for him to satisfy his sex needs, he continued to talk with Zahra on the phone more than once and each time she asks him to meet and sleep together he finds an excuse for not to see her, at the end she stopped calling him.

After the meeting with Zahra on Thursday, Shawkey was waiting eagerly for his meeting with Aida on Sunday and wondering how things will go on that meeting. On Friday Aida called Shawkey to reassure the meeting on Sunday, he told her how he was anxious to see her, she told him that she was worried form this meeting, the phone call ended after Shawkey assured Aida that everything will be alright. On Sunday Shawkey waited for Aida at the agreed location at (1.30 pm), when he saw her, she was walking and signed to him to follow her by the car until she got to a safe place where no one was there, he approached her in the car and she got inside, then he drove towards the public park, in the way Aida removed her Hijab and told Shawkey (you are handsome) he replied (you are beautiful too), Aida was a white girl (that what Shawkey likes), has black long hair reaches her chest, has brown eyes, (160) tall (near Shawkey's height 163 cm), she was slim with sexy curvy hip, there were some remains of spots on her face, but nothing serious, her eyes were big brown beautiful, her nose a bit big, but generally attractive. When they reached the park , both sat on a bench and Aida was trying to attract Shawkey's attention to the beauty of her body to take his attention away from the spots on her face (she did not has confidence in herself) , she lifted her school uniform above her knee to show him her sexy white legs and she was successful, just looking to her sexy legs made Shawkey horny, he said to her (you are really sexy in all the right areas), she was happy with his compliment , they talked general conversation, then after half an hour, Aida asked Shawkey to take her back home, so that she do not get late and make her parents worry where she will have to explain her lateness , Shawkey took her back to an area near her home and she left the car to walk back the remaining distance on feet. After this meeting Shawkey was very attracted to Aida and her sexy body and wanted eagerly to sleep with her. When Aida called that evening he tried his crafty style to convince her to sleep with him, first he thanked her for going out with him and praised her beauty, he told her how much he was attracted and admired her and her sense of humour, she told him that he was handsome and has sense of humour, too. Then he said to her (I am dying to sleep with you) she said surprisingly (is this part of our friendship) he said (I told you from the beginning, I want our friendship to be opened, without conditions or limits, we leave matters take its course) she said (and what if I got pregnant) he said (having sex will not necessary need for the man to enter his penis completely inside the female, he can just rub it with her vagina or do not enter it fully inside her, also he can put it inside her bottom, both parties will enjoy and the girl will not lose her virginity) she said (and how you knew all of that, you must have slept with many females) he said (you are the first girl in my life, I have never slept with any one before, these information I learned it from my friends, they have girlfriends) she said (then why not you ask your friends to introduce you to a girl from their girlfriends, so that you sleep with her) he said (first I do not like to ask this sort of thing from my friends, secondly you are the first girl in my life and I want to try this matter with you) then he said (you want me to sleep with another girl and maybe I get attached to her, do you want that) she said (no, I do not want you to sleep with any girl) he said (then what to do, I am attached to you and cannot get you out of my head) she laughed and asked (and this sex will require us to take off our clothes) he said (of course, then how we will do it) there was a pause, then she said (I accept, but I will take off my school uniform only, I will not take off my under wear or bra or anything else) he said (I want to see your beautiful tits and body, but never mind we will leave the matters take its course and I will not force you to do anything that you do not want to do, I want you to be willing yourself to sleep with me, everything like you wish) she said (how everything to my wish and you tell me that you want to sleep with another girl) he said (I said that I want to sleep with you and that what I want eagerly, but if you refuse I will be forced to look for another girl to sleep with her) she said after a short pause(I do not know what to say, I want to think about it) he said (good, this is a good answer, think about it and give me the result tomorrow when you call me) she asked (what if my answer was no) he said (I am attached to you now and I cannot change that, your refusal will make me sad, do you want to break my heart) she said (no, I will think about it), after that they said good bye to each other and the phone call ended. Shawkey knew that he was gambling, if Aida stopped calling him, he will lose her, because he did not know her number and she was the only attractive girl that he has, Zahra he forgot her and do not want her anymore, he was hoping that his charm and qualifications will make Aida does not risk losing him and accept to sleep with him. In the next day Aida called him, he was waiting for her call eagerly and was very worried, she said (I thought too much about the matter and made up my mind, I must be mad to make this decision, I agree, but I will not take off all my clothes, only my outside dress) he was feeling victories and said (like you wish, we will leave the matter to its time and see how it goes) she laughed and said (I do not know how you convinced me, if this was another person I would hanged up the phone on his face and do not call him again, but you are devil and have a naughty style of convincing) he laughed and said (and you are naughty girl with lovely sense of humour, you stuck inside my head and I cannot get rid of you) both of them were laughing, then he said (I want to suck your beautiful tits and nipples until they become red) she replied (you can suck them but do not hurt them, because they are delicate), they continued the phone call which now become a sexy one , then she told him that she will skip school on Thursday and wait for him in a place away from the school at eight o'clock in the morning (which was her starting school time) and he needs to pick her up to come to his home, then at (1.30 pm) he needs to bring her back to her home, so that her parents do not know about her absence from school and think that she had finished her school normally, he agreed to that.

Thursday came, Shawkey went to meet Aida at eight o'clock, she was waiting for him in her school uniform and in an isolated place as agreed, she got into his car and as soon as they left her area, she removed the Hijab, her area (Hai al-amel) was forty five minutes drive from Shawkey's area (Al-kafa'at), when they got to Shawkey's house, Shawkey started showing his house to Aida, she liked it and said that her parents want to move to another posh area suitable for their financial standard (her father was tyres dealer) and they were thinking to move to Al-ameria, which was near Shawkey's area about five minutes drive, then she said (in the future I can come walking on my feet) they both laughed. They sat in his room on the edge of the bed, Shawkey offered to make tea or juice, Aida wanted juice, he gave her juice and he drank tea, after that they were looking at each other, Shawkey took off his shirt and trousers, Aida was shy and smiling, she said (you are in a hurry Mr.), he laughed and said(we want to get use of time, Aida started opening the buttons of her school uniform and sat on the edge of the bed with her under dress on, then Shawkey helped her to get in the bed and covered her, then he took off his vest and pants, while both under the duvet, he tried to take off her under dress, she stopped his hands and said (We said that I will keep my under dress on) he replied(does not matter you are covered any way), he took off her under dress, then tried to take off her bra, she helped him to that, when he tried to take off her knickers she held her knickers with her hands and said (no, I will not take off my knickers) and kept on holding her knickers, he said(you are under the cover, and do not worry I will not put it inside you), she stopped holding her knickers and Shawkey took it off, then he removed the cover to see her body, it was a piece of art, white, slim and sexy, her breasts were round and solid, a bit bigger than orange size, her nipples were dark pink no one had touched it before, her hip and thighs were round and hairless, her pussy was small surrounded with bushy hair which made it delicious, her body was perfect, pure and untouched. When Shawkey removed the cover, she kept looking to the roof of the room, maybe she was afraid and did not know what to do, then he started to kiss her mouth, she did not know how to kiss him, but was responding to him, then he slowly went down and started to kiss her tits and suck her nipples which made it firm, her tits were firm, spongy, standing and declaring that it were there to stay, Shawkey continued to kiss and suck her tits, then he went down to her pussy, her eyes were closed, then he started to play his tongue with her clits quickly, he felt the juice coming from her vagina and became wet, her body started to be shaken like having soft electrical shocks , her vagina was filled with juice, Aida was stand still like in a coma with her eyes closed, after he felt the sweet taste of her juice, he held his iron solid cock and started rubbing it with her clits, rub it up and down, there were small batches of juice coming out of her vagina while he was rubbing his cock until a big batch came, her vagina was completely wet, Shawkey was rubbing his cock in a slow movements to enjoy as much as possible this sexy feeling, then when he reached his climax, he could not hold himself more and ejected his seamen in tissues and went to the bath room to wash his penis. When he came back he went inside the bad with her, then she opened her eyes like she came back to life from a coma and said (that was very tasty) then she said (I want to go to the bath room to wash) she got out of the bed without clothes, Shawkey was looking at her wonderful body and medium size sexy bottom and went to the bath room. While she was in the bath room, she called Shawkey, when he came to her, she told him that she wants juice with a bit of sugar, she thinks that her blood pressure went down, he brought her the juice and she drank it, she became more lively, then both of them went to bed. After ten minutes Shawkey's cock was hard again, he showed it to Aida which made her laughed and said (let us do it again), this time Shawkey put his cock inside her arsehole in doggy position, he started to push it slowly inside her, he did not face a big difficulty pushing it, it was nice feeling, so he kept on hitting her inside out nicely, her eyes were closed, he kept on hitting her until he came, he also ejected his cum in tissues and went to wash it. When he came back both of them stayed in bed, then they moved naked inside the house and went back to his room. After half an hour his cock was hard again, Aida was laughing from its sight and said while smiling (this damn thing never get tired) Shawkey said (it is not its fault, your body is the reason) she laughed again and said (and what shall I do for him now) Shawkey said (I want you to suck it), then he taught her how to do it, she started sucking it in a wonderful way until it was about to eject and same Shawkey ejected it in tissues, by now Shawkey started feeling a bit tired, so he sat on the bed to restore his strength, at about (12.45 pm) both decided to wear their clothes, so that Shawkey take Aida back to her home, when they were about to leave, Aida said (let us do it again before I go home) both of them took off their clothes again and Shawkey rubbed his cock with her clits and pussy until he came for the fourth time, then they wore their clothes, he gave her a long kiss and took her back. When Shawkey came back to his home, he was like a corpse, he could not move his legs, and he lay on the bed and went into deep sleep. In the evening Aida called Shawkey and said (I have enjoyed very much today sleeping with you, when I went home I was walking with difficulty, because of the pain between my legs) he said (I am also feeling like I am dead, I cannot walk on my legs) she laughed and said (good, so that you do not say again that I will look for another girl) he said (I think you are good enough to take all my strength) both laughed and continued with their conversation until it ended. Aida continued to call Shawkey, he tried always to arrange another meeting, at the end she agreed to meet him on another day, like the first meeting, she skipped school and he met her away from school to take her to his house, but this time and before she start taking off her clothes, she said (I am here to take off the work clothes and sleep with you, then I wear it back again to go home), she meant that she was a whore come and take off her work clothes to have sex then she wear it again and go back home, he said (do not say that, we love each other that is why we sleep together), they had sex and before he take her home she said (I will show you which house that we will buy in Al-ameria), they went to Al-ameria and she pointed out the house that her parents decision was made on, she said (this house we will buy, remember that), then he took her back home. After couple of days of their second meeting Aida mood was changed, she told him that her school had contacted her parents about her absence for two days because of her sickness, as she told them, her parents started questioning her about these days and she faced difficulty explaining to them that she was sick and came back home, then she told Shawkey that she cannot see him again, because she felt that she was wasting her time with him and he was not serious, he only wants to sleep with her, Shawkey tried to convince her otherwise and make her changing her decision, but it was in vain, she did not call him again. The problem was that Shawkey did not know her phone number only the house that they will buy.

Few weeks past and the hormones reached its peak, his problem was that he tried the sex now and got used to it, now everything was stopped, he was very horny. One day while Shawkey was in his bed, the phone rang, there was woman voice on the other side, she said (I want to speak with Mahmood please) Shawkey replied politely (sorry, there is no one here with name Mahmood) then he hanged up, then he started thinking quickly (was this a wrong number or a woman likes to play with men like Aida did, she was not Aida definitely, may be one of her friends, but no, Aida was the jealous type she will not give his number to another girl, ok if she called again I will try play with her), while Shawkey was thinking the phone rang again, he picked up the phone and said(hello)the same voice said (hello, I want to speak with Mahmood please) he said (hello, this is you again, I am sorry there is no one with the name Mahmood here, can I help you) she said (and who are you) he said (I am Shawkey and I am engineer, who are you) she said (my name is Sadia) then she asked (and are single or married) he said (I am single and still continue my study for master degree) she said with admiring voice (hellooo, means you are educated man) he said with a smile (you can say that, and you, are you single or married) she said (widow, my husband killed in the war), she meant Iraq – Iran war which was still ongoing for its eight year, then Shawkey asked (and who is Mahmood) she said (he is a friend I knew him some months ago) he said (and how is your friendship if you do not mind me asking) she said (he visit me at home and bring me all my needs, he is a soldier in the republican army who are responsible for protecting the president) Shawkey thought a bit of time, he was saying to himself (her friend was in the republican army, those people nobody can speak with them and he can cause a lot of problems to Shawkey, he must act carefully), then he asked (do you sleep with him) she said (yes, at the beginning he was very kind to me, love me and I loved him, he is big like a gorilla and when he want to have sex with me he carry me with his arms and throw me on the bed like a toy and stay with me in bed for a long time) he asked (then what is the problem) she said (I think that he is cheating on me with other girls, so I decided to cheat on him) he said (this is not right, he should not cheat on you after you trusted him and gave him your body, it is very ugly), Shawkey was speaking in a crafty way, he wanted to convince Sadia that he was a genuine person and supporting her, she said with sadness (yes, it is ugly thing and painful), then he asked (have you cheated on him yet) she said (no, not yet, I was sitting today and decided to make random calls to talk with any single man) he asked (do you like us to be friends, talk with each other and meet when you are bored) she said (I do not mind, what is your number, I am not sure of the number) he gave it to her and asked (do you like to give me your number) she said (I prefer not to give it to you, may be you call and he is there, he is very jealous person if he suspected me talking to any man, he will beat me or even kill me, he is a violent person) Shawkey said (I do not want any harm comes to you, I do not want your number, you call me when you like) she said (alright) he asked (describe yourself to me) she said (I am not white and not brown in between, I have black long hair and brown eyes, but I am a bit big) he said (you mean a bit overweight) she said (yes, I was slim in the beginning, but after giving birth to my son I started eating a lot from boredom and my weight grew) he said (how old your son) she said (two years) then they talked about her dead husband in the war that does not want to finish and the victims, there was no house left in Iraq without a martyr (as they called) and the phone call was ended. Sadia called Shawkey two more times, in the second call he told her that he wanted to sleep with her, she agreed and they arranged a meeting to pick her up with her son and bring her to his house, she said that she will give her son milk to go to sleep then they can sleep together. At that day Shawkey brought her with her son to his house, the three of them sat in his room, she gave her son his milk bottle, he kept on drinking till he fall to sleep, Sadia was a woman twenty six years old, has black long hair reached her waist, have brown eyes and she was fat, that will not matter as long he have sex with her, after her son slept on a cushion on the floor in Shawkey's room, she went inside the bed without taking off her clothes and from under the cover she took off her knickers, while Shawkey took his clothes completely then went under the cover, she said (from the way that you took off your clothes I can say that this was not your first time, you must had slept with many girls before) he answered her knowing that there was no point of lying (I use to have a friend in the past, we had a disagreement and we did not see each other anymore), then Shawkey sat on top of her and opened her legs, then he pushed his cock inside her pussy, this was the first time that Shawkey fully penetrate a female, it was a lovely feeling, at the same time he took out one of her tits from her bra to squeeze it and sucking it, he started hitting Sadia slowly at the beginning to feel that pleasure of having his cock rubbing her vagina from inside, he continued fucking her and started feeling her inside was wet and getting wetter , he started hitting faster and faster until he got to his climax, he got his cock outside her pussy and came in tissues, he definitely did not want to eject inside her and get her pregnant, after he came Sadia said (you are a strong man you can control yourself and take it out before coming), Shawkey did not know if this was a compliment or sarcasm, because he does not want to involve himself with her, then Shawkey went to the bath room to washed. Regardless of the nice feeling that he felt when he entered Sadia, he did not feel comfortable, because Sadia was looking at him all the time he was fucking her, or may be her size or because she did not take off her clothes while he was bare naked which made him embarrassed or may be because of all these reasons, therefore he did not has a wish to have sex with her any more. Then while they were in bed Sadia asked him if he wants to have more sex, he told her that he was tired may be because he did not have sex for a long time, then she got out of the bed, checked on her son and went to the bath room. Shawkey made tea for both of them, then she told him that she want to go back, he took her to an area near her home, so that no one of her neighbours see her getting out of a stranger male car and tells Mahmood about it, then Shawkey went back home. Next day Sadia called Shawkey and told him that one of her neighbours in the street had saw her getting out of his car, she told him that Shawkey was one of her relatives, then she told Shawkey that because she was afraid from Mahmood anger and that he may try to look for him, she was unable to continue with him and stop their friendship, Shawkey told her that as long she was alright that was enough for him, he does not want any harm to come to her and he accepts her decision and the phone call was ended. Actually Shawkey was not comfortable for the whole matter, there were too many risks and definitely he did not want any problems with this gorilla Mahmood, and that how his friendship with Sadia ended with one meeting only.

Chapter 5

At (1988) Shawkey entered his second year in his master study, it was the eight year of Iraq –Iran was, which a million people were killed from Iraqis and Iranians, there were thousands of widows like Sadia who lost their husbands, brothers and fathers, the percentage of males became less than the percentage of females in the society this created adultery and moral values dropped, specially with less men providing for their families and shortage of food, females started selling themselves for money to buy food or sleeping with food agents to give them a little more of rice above their share, the war itself became more dirty, because of the stubbornness of two men Saddam and Khomeini, on Iraqi TV they show (Ali Al-majid) who was cousin of Saddam, kicking and hitting Iranian war prisoners with the end of AK-47 after they had surrendered to increase the hatred of the public against them, he also was called(Ali Chemical), because he was in charge of the northern Iraqi army and authorised the use of chemical weapons on the Kurdish villages to wipe them out, thousands of them were killed. In Iran the Khomeini was brain washing his followers the Iranian militia before sending them to the battle ground, he use to give them (heaven keys) to open the gates of heaven if they killed in the war, the army use to use them to explode mines, they send them like sheep to walk over the Iraqi mine fields to clear them with their bodies before the army attack, the problem was that there were many thousands of these militia who already have the keys to flats and houses in heaven, if these flats were filled, will there any flats left for the other good people on earth to enter heaven, also how each one of these militia will know his flat, were these flats numbered or carry the names of the owners of the keys, was there post code, how they will receive their mail, too many questions. I know this may look like sarcasm and may offend some people who I apologise to them, I wanted to show the mentality of those people who were brain washed and taught that if you go and kill Iraqis and died in the process they will enter heaven, no they will not enter heaven but hell because they were killing Muslims like them, it was mentioned clearly in Quran that Muslims must not kill any soul, how about Muslims fight or kill other Muslims, both Iraqis and Iranians were Muslims, so how these militia will go to heaven, just non sense. After these militia clear the mines, the Iranian army will attack the Iraqi positions, where they will face hundreds of machine guns waiting to spree them, artillery shells, airplane rockets, basically to reach the Iraqi front lines thousands of them will be killed, then the Iraqis will attack back and get their positions back after killing more of them, just waste of lives and men, similar to the trenches fighting during the first world war.

This year Shawkey had lost all his girlfriends, he became horny, once while he was talking with his friend Hazem, he told him that he do not have girlfriends at that time, Hazem told him that he wants to leave his girlfriend Warda, because he got other new girlfriends, he offered to Shawkey to take her, Shawkey accepted, then Hazem told Warda that Shawkey was admiring her and would like to talk with her and he do not mind that, then he gave Shawkey her phone number and agreed on a fake name that Shawkey will use when calling Warda so that she knows that he was Shawkey. Shawkey called Warda, he did not know her voice, when he mentioned the fake name , she knew him and said (Shawkey) he said (yes, and you are Warda) she said (yes), he gave her his phone number and told her to call him when the time was suitable for her and the call ended. After half an hour she called him and asked (how are you) he said (fine, and you) she said (fine) then she said (Hazem told me that you want to talk with me) he said (yes, since I saw you the first time with Zahra I admired you, but could not do anything because my date was with Zahra) she said (that is right, Zahra keep on asking about you, are you seeing her at all) he said (no, after I saw you I did not want to continue with Zahra) she laughed and said in a naughty way (admiring from first sight) he said (yes, but because you was seeing Hazem I could not interfere between you two) she said (Hazem is just a friend to me there is nothing between us, I have not seen him for a long time, because he is busy with his study), Shawkey said in his mind (busy in his study my arse), then he said (I know that his study is difficult), then she said (or maybe he found another girl to talk with her) he said (I do not know about that, I do not ask him about his private matters) she said (anyway he is just a friend and I am not bothered about his females affairs), then they talked generally about his and her studies and at the end of the call he said (do you like us to be friends) she asked (how friends you mean) he said the same old story (I want our friendship to be open, we talk and get out when we have the time and if we like each other we can sleep with each other), Warda was in a good mood at that time from the effect of the phone call, so after Shawkey said his suggestion, she laughed in a naughty way and asked in a questioning way (sleep together) he said (yes, I admire you very much and like to sleep with you) she said (and this is part of our friendship) he said (yes, because it is an open friendship and without ties) she said (I will think about it) he said (good) then the phone call ended after they agreed that she will call him later. Next day Shawkey told Hazem about what happened including the sex part, he laughed and told Shawkey to be careful, because Warda was a naughty clever girl not stupid. Two days past then Warda called Shawkey, they greeted each other, when Shawkey asked her about the sex, she told him that she agree and they agreed to meet on a day in that week, Shawkey knew her area a bit far from his area near Zahra's area. On the agreed day Shawkey brought Warda to his home, Warda was a brown girl, she had cut her black long hair (since he saw her with Zahra) shorter, now it reach her collar, she have brown eyes and slim. When they got home they sat on Shawkey's bed, he told her that he will leave the room for her to take off her clothes and he will come back. After five minutes he came back , her clothes were on the chair and she was under the cover of the bed, he took off his clothes and joined her in bed, he found that she had took off all her clothes except her knickers, he removed it and removed the duvet, her body was brown, small and slim, her tits were smaller than orange size even her pussy was smaller than any other one he saw before and was shaven, then he started kissing her mouth and went down to her tits, he kissed, sucked and squeezed them, then he started rubbing his cock with her clits until he came, he washed his penis and came back to her in bed. After ten minutes he asked her if she likes to do it again, she agreed, this time he wanted to fuck her arsehole, when he tried it was very small to the size of his cock, he tried more than once, but no success, so he stopped because he did not want to injure her, he told her that he will do it from the front, he repeated the process from the front until he came. After he came back from the bath he asked her if she enjoyed the sex, she replied (yes, and you) he said (very much) and kissed her on her forehead, then he returned her home and he came back to his home. Warda kept on calling Shawkey, but he kept on thinking of Aida and passing near the house that Aida told him that her parents will buy it in Al-ameria. All the times the outside door of that house was closed, but one day while Shawkey was passing in front of the house, the gate was opened, he stopped the car and saw Aida and her sister were washing the garage, she was astonished to see him, she smiled to him and he smiled back, then he continued driving the car. That evening Aida called him and asked (how you knew my address) he said (you told me the last time we met) she said (that is right and you did not forget it) he said (how I forget it, I never stopped thinking of you) she said (me too), then she said that they had moved to the new house two weeks ago and she changed her school to a new one in Al-ameria, then they spoke about the past period and how it was difficult for both of them and now they are back friends again. After Aida return Shawkey did not see Warda again, in fact he did not see her again since the first time they had sex, Aida return was enough for him and Warda calls became less and less then stopped. About Aida he continued talking to her on the phone and met her twice, once there were celebrations at her school, she skipped the school and came to his home, they slept together and the second time he went to Aida house and slept with her and this is what happened. At one evening at about ten o'clock she called him and told him that her parents had travelled to Najaf city in the south of Iraq (which was about two hours drive from Baghdad) and she was alone at home with her sister and uncle, they are both sleeping upstairs and she was alone downstairs, so Shawkey offered to come and see her, she agreed, then he told her (leave the house outside gate open and the house entrance door open, too) she said (alright) he said (I will come riding a bicycle because the family car is with my father) she said (alright, but close the outside gate when you come in and leave the bike near the gate) he said (alright). It was winter and the sky was raining heavily still Shawkey took the bike and cycled to Aida house, despite of all the risks that someone may see him entering Aida house at (11 pm) and may call the police reporting a burglary, Shawkey entered her house, she was waiting for him in the guest room downstairs , when he arrived he was soaked with water from the rain, he took off his clothes and she gave him her robe to wear and get warmed, she operated the gas heater and both sat in the guests room, she said (you must be mad to come in this weather) she was smiling to him, he smiled to her and put his right hand inside her robe to hold her tit, she took his hand off her tit and said (you cannot sit without touching something) he laughed and she was smiling, after ten minutes when Shawkey felt warmer, she led him to her bedroom where she slept on the bed and opened her robe, although it was dark, her white gorgeous body was clear to him, his cock was hard like iron since he saw her, then he started rubbing it with her clits and pussy, she became wet while she moan, he kept on rubbing it until he came, he ejected his cum in tissues, then she told him to throw the tissues out on his way home. Shawkey did not have sex for second time because the situation was very risky, if her uncle awake he would kill them both. Shawkey wore his clothes after it was dried a bit, he kissed Aida and went back home. After half an hour she called him to make sure that he got home safely, he thanked her and the phone call ended. Aida kept on calling Shawkey till one day she told him that she was engaged to one of her relatives, it was arranged marriage and that she cannot see him again, he wished her good luck, he knew that he cannot do something about it, because his mother will tell him that he was still a student taking his pocket money from his parents and cannot look after her, besides that he was engineer and she have not even finished her secondary school, he just felt sad and helpless and he lost her.

Shawkey continued in his study and at that time the Iraq – Iran war was ended, Iran had accepted to seize fire, but they have not had agreement yet about the borders, Saddam after few months had agreed to accept Algeria treaty which what Iran wanted from the beginning and accepted to give half of Shatt Alarab river to Iran which he refused to do at the beginning, therefore a million people died for nothing , he did that because he wanted to close his eastern war front with Iran and open another one in the south with Kuwait.

Chapter 1

At the beginning of January (1989) Shawkey had graduated from the University of Technology and got his master degree in Engineering Management , therefore he was able to give lectures in the University and other educational institutions, he applied to give lectures in engineering drawing at the University of Technology and give Metallurgy engineering lectures at the Institution of Technology, he was accepted in both and started giving lectures, he tried to give as much as possible lectures to collect as much money as he can, at this time his father Karem had retired from working as accountant in a government company and found a job in a private company which imports and distributes cigarettes, it was owned by one of his relatives who belongs to a famous and rich family in Iraq they called (Al-damerchy), his family left Iraq when the Ba'ath party came to power, they were afraid that the government will take their money in the name of socialism like they did with other families, but at this period Al-damerchy family started importing and selling cigarettes in Iraq as an agreement with Uday son of Saddam where part of the profit goes to him, so they established a branch for cigarettes trade in Iraq (their main trade centre was in Jordan). Karem found a job with them, he was responsible for managing the branch in the absence of Al-damerchy oldest son (Ahmed), who was responsible for managing the branch, he use to travel between Iraq and Jordan to organise the trade. Shawkey's mother Samera also retired and opened a shop for selling food and domestic supplies, she also got a permission to supply the food shares to the residents of that area like rice, oil, sugar, milk, meat ..etc. Shawkey continued to give lectures, there was no improvement in his sex life.

Iraq – Iran war had left Iraq exhausted military and economically, there were billions of debts to European and Arabic countries like Kuwait and Saudi Arabia where they loaned Iraq money to buy weapon during the war with Iran, Saudi Arabia had accepted to forget about its loans and considered it paid, but Kuwait wanted Iraq to repay its loans to them, people says that there was a rough argument between the Iraqi delegations and Kuwaiti delegations when the Iraqis went to discuss the loans matter, this had infuriated Saddam which made him decided to invade Kuwait, but the Ba'ath party story stated that the Kuwaiti oil fields were connected under the ground with the Iraqi Oil fields in the south, so the Kuwaitis were stealing the Iraqi oil, whatever the reason was Saddam had decided to attack and invade Kuwait to add the whole country to Iraq, so first he ended the animosity with Iran and gave them Half of Shat Al-arab river which the whole war was about it, then he started prepare the army for the invasion of Kuwait. Shawkey was called to service in the army again after only one year and some months of being civilian and teaching in the University, the pressure on Al-hakem family was still there, Shawkey's cousin was jailed because he refused to work in a chemical weapons factory, Shawkey's family were monitored, in one day the Ba'ath party office in his area send people to enquire about the where about of Shawkey and if he was still studying or joined the army, his family told them that he joined the army.

When Shawkey joined the army he was sent to Al-rashid military camp to train him on using AK-47, then he was sent to Kirkuk which was a city in the north of Iraq, it has a big military camp, his unit was an engineering unit for building military shelters in the middle of Kirkuk big military camp, his unit consisted from officers and soldiers most of them were engineers, an engineer major in charge of the unit, all other officers were engineers and most of the soldiers were engineers. Shawkey's second military service was hateful and boring like the first one, not much happened during it except two incidents. The war between Iraq and the collision forces was like a game, Iraq was using primitive military weapons compared to America and the rest of the collision forces, they used the most advanced weapons including air power, when Shawkey used to meet soldiers who were on holiday and based in the south of Iraq, they used to tell him how the American air planes bomb them heavily in the south, no one dare to raise his head or these air planes throw items like pens or small toys which explode when being touched by the soldiers, they said that moral were very low there was no air cover for them and they were under the mercy of the air strikes, also many of them when they come back home for their monthly holiday they do not return to their posts, the only two times where the Iraqi air planes flew to face the American fighters in both cases they turned their direction to Iran, landed their and requested political asylum, Iraq was opened to Collision forces airplanes without any challenge.

The two incidents that occurred to Shawkey were as follow, once while Shawkey was in his unit in Kirkuk, the alarm sounded for an air strike, after a short period he saw with the rest of his unit one of the collision forces fighters in the sky, it was very far and its size looked like a fly, then this bloody fighter started hovering in circles above them preparing to attack, the horror started, everyone was running everywhere like mad people looking for a shelter, there were three shelters that the soldiers dug in the ground covered with wood (really cannot protect them even from a hand grenade) each can accommodate three soldiers, Shawkey run to the nearest one, there were four people there and because the minutes were running fast and the situation were critical, he put his head under the shelter wooden roof while his whole body was still outside, after two seconds he heard a loud bang he had never heard something like it before, then there was a silence period for a minute and the alarm sounded to declare the end of the air strike. It was clear later on that the strike was aimed to hit Kirkuk military airport and it destroyed it, the sight of the frightened soldiers and their mad dispersal was funny to the observer, but sad too shows how this war (that Saddam started like the one before) was not compatible between the two parties. The second incident occurred as follow, once the Major called the soldiers to speak with them, he told them that the unit was ordered to move to the south to make shelters there in the desert near Al-nasiriyah city, they must prepare, then he said (you all are engineers, I do not want to lose any one of you, if you find yourselves facing the Americans, there is only one direction to go and that is the American, surrender to them, this war is not yours) actually all the soldiers in the unit were already made up their minds to surrender, no one was having apatite to fight, no one believed in the causes of the war, Saddam started it for his own glory to show himself fighting the American. The next day Shawkey's unit moved south, they reached Al-nasiriyah at night, they spent the night in an empty school and in the morning they moved to the desert to start digging. The process of digging and building the shelters lasted several days, in one day while the digging process was going on the Major, the officers and the soldiers were all present, Shawkey saw a big bomber surrounded by six fighters flying above them in its way to bomb Baghdad, suddenly one of the fighters left the group and started hovering in circles above them, the Major immediately shouted for everyone to disperse, he run in one direction and everybody run in all the directions, it was another panic station sight, only this time the fighter did not attack them and went back to the rest of the group, may be the pilot was taking pictures to their positions to be bombed later, the sight of everyone running in all direction was funny and sad at the same time. After they finished building the shelters, the unit moved north to its base in Kirkuk military camp. Shawkey went to his home at Baghdad for his monthly holiday for a week, in the last day of his holiday while he was preparing his stuff to go back to his unit in the north, one of the unit officers called him and told him that the Kurdish militia had attacked Kirkuk camp and took control of it including Shawkey's unit, they had received orders to dismantle the unit and he should stay at home until further orders received. The news were delightful to Shawkey, he do not have to go there again for the moment and avoid any risks accompany that, but at the same time he was suffering from the horror that all Baghdad people were suffering from the bombing of collision forces bombers, in each air attack Shawkey and his family use to sit under the table in the living room afraid that roof may fall from the bombing, the house was not very far from Al-taji military camp north of Baghdad, so when the camp was bombed, Shawkey's house shakes like a tree, specially the sound of impact of the bombs on the ground, it was terrifying feeling.

The war did not last long after that the Iraqi army was defeated and withdrew from Kuwait, as shown around the world the poor soldiers were running for their lives on their feet, running away from the bullets and shelling of the collision forces, Iraqi army lost in this war (100,000) dead, still it was much lesser than the civilians killed by Saddam republican army and his security forces when the revolutions of the Shi'a occurred after the war, his son in law (Saddam Kamel) killed (300,000) civilians when he cracked down the revolution. When operation desert storm (Kuwait war) finished, Iraq was in chaos, lack of order and security, the police force was dismantled , some of them went to hide after the revolution started, the army was dissolved, only left the republican guards army which was loyal to Saddam and his special guards which was responsible for his protection and safety, with no law and order small groups started enter Iraq from the border with Iran, they were mostly Iraqis people who Saddam threw them out of Iraq when the war with Iran started, these groups went south of Iraq to the Shi'a cities and started the revolution against Saddam, many Shi'a people joined them including Shi'a soldiers who deserted the army, they attacked the police stations and security offices belonging to the regime and killed them with cruelty, then they took control of these cities, they declared the fall of Saddam and their freedom from his regime. At this time Iran radio was supporting them, because they were Shi'a, besides the hatred to Saddam from the Iranian for lunching war against them in the past, also to encourage the Shi'a to create a Shi'a government in Iraq. Saddam situation as follow, he lost his war with America and lost his glory, he did not make any geographical gains with his war with Iran, Iraq was on ruins military and economically with billions of dollars dept to Europe and Arabic countries, he was hated by the Iraqi people for losing thousands of their sons in the two wars, he was hated by his neighbours Iran, Kuwait, Saudi Arabia and even Egypt, because he removed all the Egyptians from Iraq and took over their properties and money, when the Kuwait war started and Egypt took the Kuwaiti side, also Israel did not escape from his animosity, he had launched several Scud missiles (ground – ground) to bring the Israeli to this war hopping that this will make the Arab people in the Arabic countries, which decided to go against him, to change their position in the war, however Israel did not fell in the trap, he knows that he was wanted internationally for the crimes he committed against the Kurds in the north of Iraq by using chemical weapons to kill thousands of them, because of all of that there was no safe place for him to go, but to stay in Iraq and fight to the last minute, so he decided to destroy the revolution and kill everyone of them. Saddam appointed his son in law (Saddam Kamel) as commander of the republican army, his job was to destroy the revolution, capture and kill all the participants, the republican army started attacking the Shi'a cities one after another, they surrender the city first and keep on shelling it continuously to weaken its resistance, then the soldiers enter the city and kill or capture all the males who left there, rape their women in front of them, as one of Shawkey's relative told him that when the republican guards entered Kerbala city (which was a holly city in Iraq) they were carrying bandanas on their tanks and armoured vehicles written on it (no Shi'a after today) to terrify the people in the city, then the soldiers started searching the houses and brought out all the males that left in the city (many families had left the city earlier running away from what was coming), they put tyres on the males and burned them alive, some were hanged using the tanks trunks , the women were raped in their homes and what were left of the men, their eyes were covered and took them in lorries to be interrogated at the security buildings in Baghdad, many of them were not seen again. At Najaf city which was also a holly city in the south of Iraq they shelled the city with Scud missiles (ground –ground), then with artillery and when the soldiers entered the city they were shooting like maniacs, the attacks by the republican army on the Shi'a cities were barbaric and brutal, however the Shi'a fighters tried ,before their cities fall, to ask help from the American forces which were not too far from them to give them weapons to fight, but the American refused, because they were on seize fire situation with the regime and supply the fighters with the weapons will break that seize of fire, this action left the Shi'a civilians under the mercy of the regime soldiers. After cracking down the revolution in the south of Iraq, Saddam sent his army to the north to destroy the Kurdish revolution there, and in same cruelty he crushed the revolution there, many Kurdish families went to the mountains on the borders with Iran and Turkey, to escape these massacres and Saddam at last crushed the revolution and killed all his opponents.

After the fighting in the Iraqi cities was over and the law and order returned under the regime, Shawkey's mother Samera suggested to Shawkey to leave Iraq, because Iraq was not a safe place under Saddam ruling, Samera and Shawkey renewed their passports, Shawkey did not put his surname Al-hakem in his passport to avoid being rejected to leave Iraq because he was from Al-hakem family, he translated his degrees and qualifications into English and authenticated it. At one day Samera returned home from the shop and told Shawkey to prepare his papers, certificates and necessary items to travel to Jordan, she had bought the tickets to travel through the desert by bus, she told him that Al-damerchy, who was a relative to his father Karem, was living in Jordan and his main cigarette trading centre was also there, they will try to see him maybe he can get Shawkey a job there, Shawkey prepared his stuff and left Iraq for the last time, he did not return ever.

When Samera and Shawkey arrived to Amman the capital of Jordan where Al-damerchy lives, she booked a room for two people in a hotel temporary until meeting Al-damerchy to see if he can employ Shawkey in his company, she gave Shawkey two pieces of gold which was a currency from Ottoman period when the Turkish used to occupy Iraq, these pieces of gold were of a great historical and monies value, she inherited it from her mother and her mother inherited it from her grand dads, she told Shawkey to protect it and safe keeping it, tell no one about it and should not be used only in emergencies. In the second day they went to Al-damerchy house, he was not there, but his wife welcomed them and gave them his company address where he was, they went to the company, he welcomed them and told Samera that his line of business was trading and selling cigarettes, he do not have factories to employ her engineer son, he said that he will see if there was any vacancy in one of his warehouses (he had several big warehouses to store his different kinds of cigarettes (Rothman, Marlboro, ...etc), then he asked Shawkey to come in the morning next day, then he reluctantly invited Samera and Shawkey to have lunch at his home, Samera thanked him and told him that they do not want to be a burden, also she have other matters to do before returning to Iraq. Samera refused the lunch offer, because she knew that it was not a genuine invitation and Al-damerchy was not enthusiast about her and her son present, in the evening she told Shawkey that she will return to Iraq in the next day, she gave him some money to support himself till he meets Al-damerchy. Shawkey went the next day to the company, Al-damerchy was not there, but his two sons Ahmed (the oldest) and Sa'eed were in the office, they welcomed him, although Shawkey felt that he was unwanted guest. After sitting an hour in the office Al-damerchy came, he welcomed Shawkey again, then he told Ahmed to take Shawkey to one of his warehouses outside Amman in Al-zarka city where he have all his warehouses, because it was cheaper for them to rent the warehouse there. Shawkey and Ahmed went to Al-zarka and the warehouse was huge, it contained several thousands of different kind of cigarettes stocked on pallets, then he started explaining to Shawkey the process of receiving the orders from the buyers, processing it, the forms need to be filled, then how to deliver these cigarettes by Lorries. After that they returned to the main office in Amman and Ahmed told Shawkey to go home and see him in the next day. When Shawkey returned to the hotel, he found another man in his room, he told Shawkey that his name was Abo Hamza, he was an Egyptian brown man in the end of his forties, he has grey hair, slim and (170) cm tall, he told Shawkey that the owner of the hotel told him to stay with Shawkey, because his room was for two people. Abo Hamza was a polite, wise man, tell jokes from time to time, so Shawkey liked him and was comfortable to stay with him in the room although he was thinking of his mother when she comes back where she will stay. In the next day Shawkey went to Al-danerchy office and sat with Ahmed till his father came, after sitting for some time, Al-damerchy told Shawkey that at the moment there were no orders or demands on the cigarettes from Iraq and generally the economical situation was not good in the whole region, so there was no vacancy available for him and that he will call Shawkey when a vacancy arise, then he asked Shawkey if he needs any money, he took (100) Jordanian Dinars to give to Shawkey, Shawkey was embarrassed and felt that Al-damercy was giving him the money as a charity, Shawkey told Al-damerchy politely with pride that he has money and thanked Al-damerchy and left the office. When he returned to the hotel he told Abo Hamza about what happened, Abo Hamza told him kindly that he does not need to worry, he will take him in the next day to his work and ask the employer if he can employ Shawkey, the job was laying marbles. Shawkey went with Abo Hamza to his work place and got a job in laying marbles, the work was physical and hard to Shawkey, he did not do this kind of work before only lecturing in the University, at the end of the working day they returned to the hotel. Shawkey became confident and trust Abo Hamza, he did not see any bad behaviour from him, and he always was kind, friendly and advising Shawkey, because he was alone in a foreign country. The next day they also went to the work as usual, they used to take their wages daily at the end of the working day, after work they returned to the hotel and Abo Hamza suggested that they will visit a friend of him in the evening, they went to his friend and everything went well, when they returned to the hotel, Shawkey was in a good mood, he told Abo Hamza about the gold pieces that he had, he showed it to him and they went to sleep. In the next morning Shawkey awoke late, Abo Hamza suppose to wake him up in the early morning to pray, then they go together to work, Shawkey did not know how to go to work he did not know Amman well, also all Abo Hamza's stuff were not there only Shawkey's stuff. Shawkey was surprised, he asked the owner of the hotel about Abo Hamza, he was told that Abo Hamza had woke up early in the morning, picked up all his stuff, paid what was left of his room rent, closed his account and left. The suspicion triggered in Shawkey's mind, he went to check his bag where the gold was, it was not there, Abo Hamza had stolen it while Shawkey was sleeping, Shawkey sat in his room sad cursing himself for being so stupid to trust a stranger and telling him about the gold, he did not listen to his mother advice not to trust or tell anyone about it, he did not know what to do, he was like a numb person whose brain stopped working and stayed in the room. At that evening his mother Samera came from Iraq to visit him and make sure that he was alright, then he told her about what happened with Al-damerchy, Abo Hamza and the stolen gold, she exploded in tears and told Shawkey with anger voice (I have told you not to trust anyone and do not tell anyone of the gold) then she said (these gold pieces were very dear and precious to me, I got it from my mother, it was the inheriting of the family), Shawkey lost the words and could not say anything, after she calmed down she went to ask the owner of the hotel about any address he knew of Abo Hamza, he told her that he did not has any address for him, then she told him about what happened, he advised her to report the matter to the police, however taking into account the period between the time where the gold was taken and reporting it to the police it gives a very slim chance to trace him, he could be anywhere, he explained to her how to get to the police station. Samera and Shawkey went to the police station to report the theft, there they took his details, but like the owner of the hotel they told her that it was too late to report it and Abo Hamza could be anywhere even had left Jordan. When they returned to the hotel Samera told Shawkey that it was not safe to leave him alone in the hotel in a room for two people, this time his gold was stolen next time he could be killed while sleeping, she must look for a room in a family house or a small flat. In the next day they looked for a flat all of them were expensive, at last they found a room in a house, the owner wanted to rent it to couples, he don't live there but visiting it from time to time to check that everything was alright and maybe he stays for a night there in a separate room for him in the house. The owner of the house was an old man and religious he agreed to rent the room for Shawkey and Samera on condition that Shawkey does not bring there any females or acts in an immoral way, because he was still a young man, Samera assured him that Shawkey was a good boy and afraid from God and will not disgrace the house. In the next day Samera told Shawkey that she will go back to Iraq and come back to Jordan soon, because she heard that Yemen needed teachers for its schools and colleges and was recruiting Iraqi teachers, she will try to find a contract for him; in the next day she went back to Iraq. One week past and Samera returned to Jordan, she told Shawkey that she could not find a contract for him, however she got the name and phone number of an Iraqi teacher there from her friend and told Shawkey that he needs to travel to Yemen and contact that teacher to get an advice from him on how to find a work, then she booked a one way ticket to Yemen for Shawkey. In his travelling day Samera was with Shawkey at Amman airport, she repeated her advices to him to be careful and do not trust anyone. When Shawkey entered the waiting room for his flight ,he looked behind him and saw his mother face was full with tears, she was waving to him, he felt that his heart sunk and felt sad for leaving her, then he went to his airplane.

Chapter 1

Yemen is a beautiful country, it has magnificent mountains views , it was not developed well the infrastructure still belongs to the late ninetieth century, most buildings and houses were old style build, transportation was also not great, but enough to suit the purpose in the country. The country has restricted traditions and Islamic rules, the traditional wearing custom of men was a dress with belt in the middle of the dress around the waist carrying a knife, females tradition clothes were black dress covered from head to feet where either the females cover the whole face or show only the eyes and sometimes they even wear gloves whatever the weather condition hot or cold, so basically males in the same family cannot identify their women if they walk in the street. There is a habit all the Yemenis have males and females and that was chewing(Khat) which is a green plant its liquid contains a drug if the person swallow it he will feel energetic for some time where he can do too many things without feeling exhausted including sex, however the person will lose his apatite to eat, because of the amount of liquid he swallows from Khat and the water that he drinks to beak the bitter taste of Khat, he will not feels hungry and that is why most Yemenis are slim like Somalis and Ethiopians because they also have the same habit of chewing Khat, the other effect of the drug was when the energetic hours finished, the person becomes feeling miserable and exhausted till the next time he chews Khat again, however the nature of all Yemenis was friendly, supportive and welcoming.

Shawkey's flight to Yemen was alright, when he arrived to Sana'a (capital of Yemen) airport, he took his suit cases and left the airport looking for a taxi to take him to the centre of the city which was several kilometres from the airport, he saw all the drivers have a bulge on one side of their faces inside it was green leaves and they were chewing it, it was not a pretty sight and look revolting (he did not know the story of the Khat at that time), he asked one of the drivers to take him to the centre of Sana'a, when he got there he looked for a room for one person in a hotel, he got one and put his stuff inside the room, went out for a meal and discovering the city, then he called his mother to assure her that he reached Yemen safely and went back to his hotel to spend the night. The Yemenis generally likes Iraqis, because they liked Saddam, they think that he was a great leader because he fought the American although he lost the war they respected him more than their own president Ali Saleh , so they always welcome passionately any Iraqi they meet. In the next day Shawkey contacted the Iraqi teacher his name was Sadoon, he greeted him and told him that his mother gave Samera his phone number to contact him when he get to Yemen to seek advice on employment, Sadoon welcomed Shawkey and invited him to visit his home to talk. Shawkey went to Sadoon home, he was living in a house with other four Iraqis, each one has his own room, but they share the kitchen, the bathroom and pay the rent together, after drinking tea and introduce Shawkey to the other Iraqis, Sadoon started talking, he said to Shawkey that the economical situation of Yemen was not good specially after the Kuwait war (first gulf war), because Yemen was supporting Saddam in the war, even the money aid that Yemen use to get from Kuwait and Saudi Arabia was stopped, all Yemenis that used to work in Kuwait And Saudi Arabia were kicked out and returned to Yemen which increased the difficulty of the economical situation and chances for getting work, they have not received their salaries from the government for three months, because the government did not have the money to pay them, but he hopes to get his salary this month as a one full payment. Then he told Shawkey that he can try to apply for the ministry of education for teaching position and wait or he can also apply for private companies for engineering work and he mentioned that Al-sa'ed company was one of the most famous companies in Yemen, they have several factories in Taiz city in the south of Yemen, they are very rich family and has business even in England, Shawkey asked Sadoon how to apply to them and he explained it to him and on how to be in touch with their main office in Sana'a. Then they started discussing the region matters, other teachers got involved and talked about the females in Yemen and how they like Iraqis and some of them make friendship with Iraqis, but secretly. Shawkey's visit to Sadoon finished, he went to prepare his certificates, made copies of them to use them with his applications for work, he would be lucky to get a job in these difficult economical times, he applied to work for the government and Al-sa'ed company and waited for an answer. During this time whenever he leaves his room to take a walk in the city, the resident of the hotel welcome him and tell him (welcome Iraqi), once while he was about to leave the hotel, there were about ten Yemenis sitting on cushions on the floor (it is a Yemeni tradition to sit on cushions on the floor instead of chairs), they were chewing Khat, they called him to sit with them and as a friendly gesture he sat with them, then one of them gave Shawkey a branch of Kaht to chew, Shawkey apologised and told him politely that he do not chew Kaht, but also as a friendly gesture he pulled one leaf of the branch and put it in his mouth, its taste was bitter and forced Shawkey to take it out, the Yemenis laughed and one of them said (this is better, so that you do not get use to it, it is expensive), then they started talking about the war and how Saddam was a hero, because he faced America and the whole world alone and asked Shawkey about his opinion, he was not sure what to say, if he says his opinion honestly, they will get upset, so he thought of answering their question in a diplomatic way and told them that Saddam should prepared his military first before fighting America, they agreed with him, then Shawkey excused them to leave to do some things and thanked them, he did not want to go into discussions about the war, because he will make them upset.

Five days past then one of Al-sa'ed family his name (Hamdon) called him and told him that he read his CV and application for work and wants to meet him, they agreed on a certain day in their office in Sana'a. Shawkey went to the interview and Showed Hamdon his degrees and experience, Hamdon accepted him to work in their main office in Taiz, he told Shawkey that he will be working from their main office in Taiz to visit their factories there, their factories were for different materials, food, plastic, cooking oil and shampoo, he also said that the company will provide Shawkey with a place to stay in their compound there, which many nationalities live there (Indians, Egyptians, Pakistanis) and a car to make him visit the factories and make improvements there whenever possible, Shawkey thanked him and agreed on a starting date.

Shawkey went to Taiz, he entered Al-sa'ed main office there which was called (the general office for managing Al-sa'ed and his sons companies) he met Hamdon who welcomed him and told the officer who was responsible for looking after the employees needs to give Shawkey the key of the flat that he will stay in, take all his stuff to the flat and supply him with whatever he needs, the employees officer took Shawkey to his flat, it was the at the ground floor of a building consists of four flats, two at the ground floor and two at the first floor, above the first floor there was a small second floor free from flats and leads to the roof which was opened like all middle east houses, on the roof there were the water tanks, the water in Yemen taken from wells and distributed to the houses once a week to fill their water tanks which should be enough for the occupants for a week till the next delivery date. in front Shawkey's flat there was another flat occupied by an Indian family consists of the wife, the husband and three children, the flat above him it was occupied by another Indian family called Patel consists of the wife, the husband and two females children, the husband was a manager in one of Al-sa'ed factories, the third and forth flat in the first floor was empty. The building was surrounded by a brick wall and there was a gate guarded by a guard, his job was to guard the gate and responds to the employees need by reporting it the employee officer. Shawkey's flat consisted from three bedrooms, kitchen and two bathrooms, he took the biggest bedroom, the flat was occupied by him only and was facing the outside gate. The conditions in this compound were no women allowed to enter it except if they were families, no one allowed to enter the compound after (11 pm) the gate will be closed and the guard go to sleep, Shawkey was informed about it. After Shawkey put his stuff in the new flat, he went out to buy his food supplies from the market which was not far from the compound, everything else was provided in the flat like pans, plates and all other cooking facilities, and then he returned to spend his night in the flat for the first time.

In the next day Shawkey went to the company office in Taiz, Hamdon introduced him to his colleague (Mustafa), who was a Yemeni engineer graduated from an American University and will be working together in his office, he worked with Al-sa'ed company for four years, then Hamdon introduced Shawkey to his line manager (Fat'hy), he was Mustafa's line manager too, he was an Egyptian engineer in the end of his forties, has grey hair and a person with two faces (as Shawkey knew later), Shawkey did not like his personality, Shawkey and Mustafa were nearly similar ages, both at the end of their twenties, Mustafa and Fat'hy were brown, but Shawkey was white, both Fat'hy and Hamdon were taller than Shawkey and Mustafa, they were about (180) cm tall, while Shawkey was (163) cm and Mustafa was (155) cm tall, after the introduction was finished, Mustafa started explaining his and Shawkey's duties in the office, it was visiting the factories of Al-sa'ed company and follow up the production process there, if there were any problems, it will be studied and discussed with the engineers and the factory manager there to resolve it, also there were monthly reports need to be produced about the production progress in the factories and presented in flowcharts to Fat'hy as their line manager who will present it to Hamdon as the general manager of Al-sa'ed company . Mustafa started taking Shawkey with him to the factories and introduced him to the managers there and showed him the kinds of products they produced to have a good idea about it before becoming independent from him. After two months Shawkey became familiar with his work, but still taking advice from Mustafa whenever needed, at this period another new graduate Yemeni engineer was employed his name (Sa'ad), he did not has any experience before and started learning the job from Mustafa and Shawkey. Mustafa, Shawkey and Sa'ad used to discuss the work matters in the office when they are there, once while they were in their discussion, Mustafa asked Shawkey about one of the houses that they pass in their way to the factories to see if he knew about its story, when Shawkey denied that, Mustafa told him that the house was occupied by (Jinn), (who were creatures God created from fire like humans were created from mud, these creatures eat bones and have supernatural powers like moving from place to place instantly, can go inside the human body and take control of it, can teach humans knowledge and protect them and many other powers, they were mentioned in Quran), so Shawkey was surprised to hear that, then Mustafa told him that the house was deserted for a long time, the owner tried to rent it more than once, but the lodgers leave it after a short period of time after the Jinn appear to them at night, since then the house was left empty and only the Jinn sounds come from it at night. Shawkey was listening to Mustafa attentively, he liked these stories about the Jinn and spirits and believed in it, then Mustafa told him that Yemen was the original Jinn land they were created there and then they moved elsewhere on earth, then he said to Shawkey (have you heard about the book called The Sun of the Greatest Knowledge), Shawkey denied that, Mustafa said (some religious men were using it in Yemen to bring Jinn, when the government knew , it was forbidden publish it and now it is rare to find), Shawkey was listening to Mustafa in a great interest, then he told Mustafa (I believe in Jinn and would be very interested to bring them and speak with them), Mustafa and Sa'ad laughed then Mustafa said (bringing Jinn is very serious matter, if you bring a bad Jinn he will enter your body and you lose your mind and yourself or even kill you, you must have very religious knowledge to protect and defend yourself, you cannot kill the Jinn with a knife or any weapon of this world, but must use verses from Quran to keep them away and protect yourself), Shawkey said (this will not frighten me, my heart is strong and I do not afraid from them), then Shawkey asked Sa'ad if he knew any religious man to talk with him about the subject, Sa'ad told him there was a religious man called (El-sheikh Al-hafthy), he was known for his religious knowledge and talking with the Jinn, his house was two floors, the ground one was made as a Mosque where his followers go there to pray , ask his blessing and solve their problems with his religious powers and the first floor was where he lives, he explained to Shawkey how to get there. Preparing and bringing Jinn was a challenging matter to Shawkey, he was a young man and liked challenges, he decided to try that, his plan was consists of two parts, the first was getting this book and read it and the second part was visiting Al-hafthy and speak with him. Shawkey started looking for the book, in each library he entered and ask about it their answer was negative or they look at him with suspicious look and tell him that it was not available, at last he found it in a small book shop and the owner of the book shop advised him to be careful when reading it. Shawkey did not tell his mother about his intensions with the Jinn, because he knew that she will object to the whole idea and prevent him from doing it, the book consists of many chapters teaching the reader how to write symbols, letters and numbers in certain sequence and shapes, also drawing geometric shapes to do different things like how to make females like you, how you get revenge and hurt your neighbour who was causing you nuisance, how to bring someone far from you to your room, how to make someone sick or cure yourself from a disease, how to bring a good Jinn to help you to resolve your needs or a bad Jinn to hurt someone else and many other things, the symbols used in the book either from ancient languages or taken from the Quran, but written in a special way. Shawkey was interested in the part concerning with bringing the Jinn, he read the requirements to do the process, fasting for several days, eating meat free food, being alone in a deserted place from humans (like he was living alone in the flat), reading verses from Quran in the night of bringing the Jinn, buying certain incenses and do it in the right time and hour, Shawkey took a week holiday from work and prepared what was mentioned in the book, in the final night he sat alone in the flat, reading the required verses from Quran and burning the incenses trying to bring the Jinn, nothing happened, he could not bring the Jinn or even a mouse.

After failing in this part of the plan maybe because he did not know the location of the planets in the sky or there was no point of doing it any way, he decided to meet Al-hafthy maybe he can help him to speak with the Jinn. Shawkey did not tell Mustafa and Sa'ad about his failed experiment to bring the Jinn, so that they do not make fun of him, after some days he asked the guard in his compound where he lives about the location of Al-hafthy house and he directed him. Shawkey's working hours divided by two parts, morning time starts from eight till twelve o'clock, then the company take afternoon break from twelve to four o'clock in the evening , the Yemenis usually use it to Chew Khat , get the energy to use it in the second part of the working day between four o'clock and eight o'clock at night , while the other employees use it to have lunch and taking a nap, so when Shawkey finished his work at eight o'clock that evening he went to Al-hafthy house, there was no one present in the mosque at the ground floor except a young male between (15 – 17) years old was looking after it, Shawkey introduced himself to the boy who called (Jafar) and told him that he want to meet Al-hafthy to enquire about a personal matter, Jafar went for ten minutes, then when he came back he told Shawkey that Al-hafthy was busy now, but he will see him tomorrow at nine o'clock in the evening, Shawkey went back home. In the next day Shawkey went to the mosque at nine o'clock, there were five adult young men in their twenties sitting in the mosque, after Shawkey introduced himself to them he sat with them on the cushions on the floor, they were Al-hafthy followers, he waited for couple of minutes, then one of the young men said to Shawkey that they will start singing a religious song to praise God and bring the angles to the mosque, he brought a small drum and started hitting it in a certain tune, the rest started singing, Shawkey was monitoring the situation and did not know what to do, he was for the first time in this kind of situation, so he did not sing or say anything, but only was smiling to them, the singing last for fifteen minutes, then they stopped, their mood was good, one of them told Shawkey (did you see how the weather changed inside the mosque, it became colder because the angles were flying over us), actually it was warm when Shawkey came at the beginning, now it was a bit colder may be because of the singing and the movements of the participants made a flow of air to change the temperature. After half an hour of waiting, Jafar came and told Shawkey that Al-hafthy will see him now, Shawkey went upstairs and entered a room full of Quran verses written on bandanas and pictures hanged on the wall, there were several Islamic trophies and vases, many candles and nice smell, Al-hafthy was sitting on a comfortable big cushion on the floor, he was white in his fifties, he had grey hair and grey beard, he was wearing a white dress, he smiled to Shawkey and told him to sit beside him, Shawkey greeted Al-hafthy and felt comfortable for his smiling friendly face, then Al-hafthy asked Shawkey(what is your need), Shawkey replied (I want to bring Jinn and speak with them, I want you to help me to bring them and I will pay your fee), Al-hafthy looked at Shawkey for two seconds, then smiled and asked (and why you want to bring them) Shawkey said (I know they have great powers and I want to take one of them as a friend to teach me knowledge) Al-hafthy turned his face from Shawkey, but still was smiling, he looked to the floor thinking, then after ten seconds he said (I have a Jinn friend, he comes to me in certain times, he is a good Jinn, I will speak with him first, I will send him to where you live to see the place and bring me the news and I will see if it is possible for you to speak with the Jinn) then he said (the Jinn will come while you are sleeping, do you want him to wake you up or not), Shawkey felt worry from the idea that he will see a Jinn in his room alone, he told Al-hafthy I prefer he do not wake me up), Al-hafthy smiled and asked (alright, where you live) Shawkey replied (in the compound of Al-sa'ed company) Al-hafthy said (I know it, I will send the Jinn tomorrow while you are sleeping, then come to see me in two days) Shawkey said (alright, how much is your fee) Al-hafthy said (do not worry about it now, let us see the result first) Shawkey thanked Al-hafthy and left. When Shawkey returned to the compound he was worried and thinking, how the Jinn will find his flat in the compound, he did not tell him which flat, will Al-hafthy help him or not, there were too many questions in his head. After two days Shawkey returned to Al-hafthy, this time he did not wait too long, Al-hafthy saw him after five minutes, when Shawkey entered the room to see Al-hafthy, he was smiling like before, Shawkey sat beside him, then the smile disappeared and said to Shawkey in a serious but polite voice(I cannot help you, the Jinn found something in your room immoral and dirty) Shawkey was taken by surprise and lost the words , he was thinking what was immoral or dirty in his room , then he remembered that he bought a sex magazine when he was in Jordan to look at it when he gets frustrated, but the magazine was well hidden in his clothes wardrobe, how the bloody Jinn found it, Shawkey was still astonished, they he said (I still do not know what is the bad thing in my room) Al-hafthy said (my advice is to continue with your present work and forget about the Jinn) Shawkey was not happy with Al-hafthy advice and said (alright, and how much is your fee) Al-hafthy said (nothing), then Shawkey thanked Al-hafthy and left the mosque and never came back. When Shawkey got back home, he checked his wardrobe and found the magazine, it was in its location the same way it was left, has not been touched or moved, there was nothing to indicate that anyone has entered his room everything was in its location, after that Shawkey left the Jinn matter, because he knew that it was a dead end.

Shawkey continued with his work in the company, he started visiting his Iraqi friends and sometimes at the weekend he travelled on Thursday after finishing his work in the company, from Taiz to Sana'a with his friends using the company car and returning on Friday evening, the road between Taiz and Sana'a was full of nice views to the mountains, sometimes he was travelling to Aden in the south of Yemen which was a seaport on the Red sea, he also went to Al-hudaydah city which was also a seaport on the Red sea, he stood on the beach and said to himself (I have never thought in all my life that I will be standing watching the Red sea, but that what was written to me). Once while Shawkey was talking with his Iraqi friends about the Yemeni Girls, one of then told him (why you do not befriend Yemeni girls, you have a car and the process is easy, girls cover their faces with vale, their fathers and brothers cannot identify them in the street) Shawkey replied that he do not know how to do it, Yemenis are restricted and the men carry knives, they told him that the men will not recognise their women, because of the vale and there are many Yemeni girls befriend Iraqis, Shawkey said I will see the situation and decide. One day Shawkey decided after he finished his morning work at twelve to go home for lunch and leave at one o'clock in the afternoon to the city to see how things were going. He was told by his friends that if he see a woman walk by herself, he only need to pass her by the car and stop, if she liked him she will ride with him, Shawkey wanted to test the theory, he went to the centre of Taiz, stopped his car and start monitoring, there were many women in the street, it was summer and the temperature was warm about twenty three degrees, the women were walking either with their children or without them in pairs, he saw a woman walking alone, there was a parked car inside it was a Yemeni chewing Khat, when she approached the car, she just got inside and the car moved. Shawkey said to himself that he will try this style, now there were no females on the street, Shawkey started driving in the city until he saw one female walking alone, he moved slowly beside her with his car, he looked quickly towards her while he was passing her; she looked at him, too. Then he stopped the car about five metres from her, when she reached his car, she opened the door and sat at the passenger front seat, at that time Shawkey moved the car in the direction of leaving Taiz city to the surrounding hills away from the eyes. While Shawkey was driving the car , he said (my name is Shawkey, what is yours) she asked (you are Iraqi) he replied (yes) she said (my name is Karema, what you do for living) he replied (engineer working with Al-sa'ed company) she said (this is good, I have not seen an Iraqi in all my life), at that time they had got out of Taiz to the surrounding hills, he stopped his car in an isolated spot and asked her to remove her vale, she removed it, Karema was a brown girl has black long hair, black eyes, (150) cm tall and a bit fat, then they started talking about themselves, he knew that she had finished her secondary school and now sitting at home, then Shawkey started suggesting to her in a naughty way to be friends, she did not like the idea, because she was looking for marriage. Shawkey did not get what he wanted in this experiment, however he knew the technique of hunting girls in Yemen, after spending half an hour talking, he returned her to Taiz and let her out of the car in the location that she wanted and went back home, he was optimistic. In the next day he done the same thing, but this time two girls got inside his car and sat at the back seat, one of them her name was Lamia and her sister name was Warda, Lamia was older than Warda, she was in her twenties, has black long hair, black eyes, (150) cm tall and a bit fat, Warda was about seventeen years old, has black long hair, black eyes, (145) cm tall and slim, both were brown, when they got to the same isolated spot and removed their vale, Shawkey wanted to sleep with both of them, so he thought that if he convince the older one he can then sleep with the younger one, he suggested the idea of friendship to them , they both laughed, then after they got use to him, he asked Lamia if she accept that he sleeps with her, she laughed and asked (and where we will sleep, here in the hills) he replied (no, I will try to rent a flat, so that we can meet there), she agreed to that, at that time Warda was smiling to Shawkey in a naughty way, then they continued talking and told Shawkey that there were many Yemeni women befriend men to get Khat and chew it together then have sex and other women sleep with the men just to get money to spend it on their children or the men take care of their families, after talking for some time Shawkey took Lamia and Warda back to Taiz, he gave his company number to Lamia to call him (he did not has a landline in his flat) and took their phone number to call them later and make the arrangement to meet when he gets the flat. Shawkey could not bring girls to his flat where he lives, because the guard will inform the employee's officer who in return will inform Hamdon about it and that can cause a serious problem to Shawkey at his work. Shawkey started looking for a flat to rent until he found a house to rent in the suburbs of Taiz, he rented it for a month and paid the rent in advance, it consisted of one bedroom, one living room, kitchen and a bathroom, he furnished it just with the necessaries like a mattress to sleep on, cushions to sit on and some hygienic and kitchen stuff. Then Shawkey called Lamia and made arrangements for a meeting, he met her that day at one o'clock in the afternoon, she was with her sister Warda and took them to the house, he stopped his car at a distance from the house and gave the key to Lamia to go to the house first with her sister and wait for him there, he did not want any of the neighbours to see him with them, because he was not wearing the traditional Yemeni custom, just a shirt and trousers which means that he was a foreigner, this will make them suspicious and tell the landlord (foreigner and two Yemeni girls what they were doing??). When he entered the house Lamia and Warda were sitting on the cushions on the floor in the living room, he asked them if they wanted tea, they thanked him and declined, then Shawkey told Lamia to go to the bedroom, in the bedroom he took his trousers off and kept his shirt on, he asked Lamia to take off her clothes, she took off her knickers only and kept her black dress on, Shawkey took Lamia tits out and started kissing her mouth and neck while squeezing her tits and sucking her nipples, Lamia was smiling to Shawkey and her both eyes were open, then he held his cock and started rubbing it with Lamia clits, after some seconds she became wet all over her pussy, he reached his climax and ejected his seamen in tissues, she laughed for that, he did not like her laughter, he felt that she was laughing about what he done, he went to the bathroom to wash, when he came back Lamia had wore her knickers and was sitting with Warda in the living room, he sat with them, but he did not show his discomfort of what happened earlier, after fifteen minutes Shawkey told the girls to go and wait near his car while he locks the house and follow them separately, then he returned the girls to Taiz to a distance from where they were living and he went back to his flat in the compound. Regardless the sex experience that Shawkey had with Lamia was not perfect comparing to the sex he had before with Aida, but it was a way to get rid of his frustration, he decided to sleep the next time with Warda, she was more attractive and younger than Lamia.

After some days Shawkey called Lamia house, this time he spoke with Warda, he told her that he want to meet her alone and sleep with her, she said (and what about Lamia, you do not want to see her, I thought you like her) he said (from the beginning I liked you, but I agreed to sleep with Lamia because she was your older sister) she said (alright, I will see alone), they agreed on a time that day. Shawkey went to his date at one o'clock, Warda was waiting for him alone, he took her to the house, they repeated the same drill getting into the house, in the bedroom Shawkey took off his trousers and pants, Warda took off her knickers and kept her outside dress, but opened the upper buttons of her dress for Shawkey to take out her tits, then Shawkey started kissing her mouth, neck, sucking her tits and nipples, Warda eyes were closed and she was quiet, her pussy was shaved and smaller than Lamia's one, he started rubbing his cock with her clits and pussy until he came, when he came back from the bathroom she was sitting waiting for him, after ten minutes he told her to take a doggy position, she did that , then he started fucking her from her bottom, at that time she was making moan sounds, he kept on hitting her bottom until he came. When he came back from washing she had wore her knickers and fixed her clothes, she was smiling to him, he thanked her and kissed her on the forehead, he told her that he enjoyed the sex very much, the time was three o'clock, he should start his work at four o'clock, so he took her back to her home and quickly went to his flat to change and go to work. After couple of days two Egyptian engineers brought to his flat, they were Mohammed and Salem, so the flat now occupied by three people, they have to share its facilities together, however each one has his own room, and the house that Shawkey rented had lost it, because one of the neighbours had seen Shawkey and Warda getting out of the house (even they were separately) and complaint to the landlord that there are females coming to the house on different occasions and the house was empty most of the time, so the land lord contacted Shawkey and told him that he took over the house and cancelled the rent, because he thought that the house was used for immoral purposes, although Shawkey tried to convince him that this was not the case and that he sleeps sometimes with his friends and that was interfering with his private matters, it did not work and Shawkey lost the house.

Days past and Shawkey stopped seeing Warda and Lamia, he entered his second year working in the company, one days one of his Iraqi friends his name was Kamal told Shawkey that he met a Yemeni girl her name was Su'ad and he needs Shawkey and his car to take her out, Shawkey told him that he do not mind, Kamal made a date with the girl on Friday, which was official holiday at six o'clock, in the exact time Shawkey and Kamal went to see Su'ad, there were two females waiting for them, when they got inside the car, Kamal was the driver, Su'ad sat at the front seat and the other female sat at the back seat with Shawkey, then Kamal took the car outside Taiz. In the way both women removed their vale and Su'ad introduced her ante Sameha to them, Su'ad was brown, sixteen years old, has black long hair , black eyes and (150) cm tall, Sameha was relatively white, in the end of her thirties, relatively attractive and (160) cm tall, both females were slim and wearing the typical Yemeni black dress and vale, Shawkey started talking with Sameha about the friendship subject and that he needs someone to talk and get out with, she was friendly and smiling to him, after half an hour of driving, Shawkey asked Sameha if it was alright for him to sleep on her lap, she agreed, then he told her (I like to hold your tit) she laughed and started undoing the top buttons of her dress, Shawkey did not waste time and put his right hand inside her dress and held her right tit while still sleeping on her lap, then he started rubbing his finger with her nipple, Sameha eyes started closing and opening she was enjoying what he was doing, Shawkey learned from his experience with Yemeni girls that they obey the man and do what they told without any objection as long as they like him, while Shawkey was playing with Sameha tit, Kamal was trying to hold Su'ad hand or thigh, but she was refusing, he told her (look what they doing in the back seat and you do not want me to put my hand on your thigh), he told her that with a sad voice, then Su'ad looked at the back seat, Sameha was smiling, then Su'ad turned her face to the front and told Kamal (they are free to do what they want), then Kamal put his hand on her left thigh, she did not object this time, but when he tried to move his hand up to her knickers, she pushed his hand again. After that Shawkey sat on his seat and continued to talk with Sameha, he gave her his phone to contact him and meet him on a different day; she did not give him her phone number. On Saturday Sameha contacted Shawkey to meet him at one o'clock, Sameha was a single female never married before, she finished her secondary school and sat at home waiting for Mr. Right, but no one knocked the door, so her relationship with Shawkey was a chance for her maybe she get a husband, her chances of getting married were getting slimmer with getting older, usually females in Yemen get married in a very early age like (14 or 15) mainly before they reach their twenty otherwise it becomes late. Shawkey took Sameha to isolated place in the hills as usual, she was sitting beside him at the front seat, he asked her to undo the upper buttons of her dress, she did that, he put his hand inside her dress and started squeezing her tits and rub her nipples, then he told her to take off her knickers, she did that, he put his hand inside her dress and pushed his middle finger inside her pussy and started to rub her clits with two fingers, he kept rubbing his fingers until her pussy was wet, Sameha at that time her eyes were closing and opening, she was enjoying rubbing her clits and pussy, she was smiling to Shawkey, then he took his fingers and smell the liquid on them, it was horny smell and lovely, then he asked Sameha to go to the back seat, they went there, he asked her to suck his cock, she agreed, she started to undo his trousers buttons and took off his cock which was at that time solid like Iron and she started to suck it, he put one of his hands behind her head to push her mouth inside out his cock while the other hand was squeezing her tits, it was a lovely feeling to Shawkey, Sameha kept on sucking his cock until he got to his climax, he took it out and ejected in tissues. After that they sat at the front seats, he thanked her and kissed her from her mouth, then he told her that at the moment he does not has a flat to meet, when he gets one he will tell her and they agreed to meet in the next week, then he took her back to a place near her home where she will continue walking to her home on feet.

Chapter 4

In this period Shawkey was treating his neighbours in the compound in a friendly manner, he greet them whenever he sees them if he was leaving or coming back from work, the married Indian female above his flat Mrs. Patel was greeting him in a friendly way too, her name was (Abani) she was a brown woman in the end of her thirties, has black long beautiful hair, brown eyes, slim and (150) cm tall, she was an attractive woman brings the eyes to her, once he met her at the ground floor in front of his flat, at that time the water supply to the flats from the water tanks on the roof was weak, she asked Shawkey (is there water in the tanks, the water in my flat is weak) he replied (in my flat the water is weak too, I went to the roof to see that there is no leaking from the tank), he was smiling to her, then he asked her innocently (and you do you has leaking in your tank), she looked in a naughty way and laughed, then she went upstairs to her flat, Shawkey was surprised from her laughter and look, he was asking himself if he had asked a naughty question, then he got it at last, that she thought he was being naughty, he was happy with that, because she laughed to him, so it is not impossible mission after all, he decided to play the leaking tune when he sees her again. In the evening Shawkey had noticed that Abani usually go out on her terrace between (10-11 pm) , may be to have fresh air or bored, so when he heard her opening her terrace door, he came out and stood under her terrace, he greeted her and she greeted him back in soft voice and said (my husband is sleeping in the next room) he asked in a soft naughty voice (did you find any leaking in the tank or it was plugged) she looked at him in a naughty magical eyes and laughed, but did not answer him, then he said (nice night, but I did not know that the moon will fall from the sky to the earth), now he was looking to her with naughty eyes, she asked in erotic way (and where is this moon) he said (on the terrace above me), she laughed and said (I am not a moon) he said (you are underestimating your beauty), then she smiled to him in an attractive way and said (and how many women you told them that) he said (you are the first woman I tell her that, and I do not have another woman), after that they kept on talking about work, she told him that her husband was a manager for one of Al-sa'ed factories, she does not work and spending her time taking her daughters to school and bringing them back, cooking and that is all, sometimes she feels bored and come out here to the terrace to have fresh air. After talking with Abani for half an hour, she told him that she will get inside, she wished him good night and he did the same and went back to his flat.

Shawkey kept on looking for a flat to rent to sleep with Sameha, at last he found a small ground floor flat in a building from two floors, then when he met Sameha he took her to the flat, same old manoeuvre he made to enter the flat, she went first then he followed her, when they were inside they sat on the cushions , then he said to her to take off all her clothes, he turned his face to make her feel comfortable, he took off all his clothes and turned his face, Sameha was totally naked, but was covering her tits and pussy with a pillow, then he sat beside her and took off the pillow and throw it away, he asked her to sleep, she slept totally naked in front of him, she has a nice slim body with round tits and small nipples, never been touched, her pussy was shaved and relatively big, he slept on her and started kissing her mouth, face, neck, then down to her tits squeezing and kissing them, sucking them, Sameha was closing and opening her eyes and making moans from pleasure, then Shawkey went down to her pussy, he opened her legs and started licking her pussy and clits with his tongue, she was moaning from pleasure, Shawkey continued to lick her until her juice start coming heavily, her pussy was completely wet, then he pushed his cock inside her pussy for a small distance (he did not want to push it inside her completely to avoid opening her and make her lose her virginity), when he pushed it inside her pussy there was a difficulty to do it, so he made it slowly inside out, clearly she has not had sex before, he continued fucking her in slow hits, then quicker and quicker until he got to his climax and ejected in tissues. Shawkey looked at Sameha, she opened her eyes and smiled to him, then he kept on kissing her again and again and asked (did you enjoyed it) she said (yes, and you) he said (I enjoyed it very much), after that they sat for ten minutes, he asked her if she likes to do it from behind, she declined that and said that she preferred it from the front, so he asked her to suck his cock, she done it perfectly until he came. When it was three o'clock they wore their clothes and he took her back to her home.

In the next day at evening around ten o'clock Shawkey heard the terrace door open, he came out and stood under Abani terrace and said (I will go up to the roof to check if the water tank is alright), she laughed, Shawkey went to the roof and waited maybe Abani will also come up, it was dark he waited for five minutes, then he started to worry maybe she will not come up, he went back to the second floor which was a small area, no flats there only light and waited for two minutes at the top of the stairs, then Abani appeared she was coming up softly, they smiled to each other and she stood beside him, then he tried to kiss her mouth, she turned her face, he started kissing her face, then he took out his tongue and started licking her ears, he heard her moan, he go down to lick her neck, she was moaning and moaning, while his tongue was busy with her neck, he tried to open her Indian custom, she held his hand with her hand, then he tried to push his hand in the gap at the back of her dress to touch her bottom, she also prevented his hand from that, then he tried to put his hand from the gap in the front of her dress to squeeze her tits, he succeeded at the end and held her right tit, it was soft, small and nice, then he pushed his finger and start rubbing her nipple, she moan again, although she was holding his hand at that time from going other places he tried to put his hand on her pussy from outside her dress to rub it, she pushing his hand away, but she kept him holding her tit and rubbing it, her moan had excited him very much and became horny, after ten minutes he stopped licking her neck, he was smiling in a horny way, she also smiled to him in the same way, then she told him that she will come downstairs first, he must wait five minutes then come down, he did that and their first meeting ended successfully. Shawkey continued grooming Abani under her terrace or meet her upstairs to excite her, but the matter did not go beyond that, because her daughters were in the flat in the afternoon, her husband were there at night and in the morning Shawkey has work, also the guard was there all the time so it was a risky business to have a full sex.

About Shawkey's work, he went one day to one of the factories of the company as usual, after he checked the production, he sat with the factory manager who was called Tahsen in his office, he was an Egyptian engineer, suddenly he started arguing with Shawkey accusing him, Mustafa, sa'ad and Fat'hy of being idiots, they do not know how to do their jobs and they were wasting their time by coming to the factories, then he accused Shawkey that he had nothing to do just coming to the factory to waste time, Shawkey was angry and told Tahsen that he will report him to his manager Fat'hy, at that time Shawkey did not know that Tahsen hates Fat'hy, there were several problems between them in the past and this attack was to degrade Fat'hy by humiliating Shawkey who was working for Fat'hy and Shawkey fell in the trap. When Shawkey went back to the office, he told Fat'hy about what happened, Fat'hy told him to write a report of the incident, so that he give it to Hamdon, when Shawkey sat with Mustafa and told him about what happened, Mustafa told Shawkey about the hatred between the two men and writing the report will make Shawkey the trouble maker who wants to create a problem between Fat'hy and Tahsen, both of them were managers and he was a new employee, at the end Tahsen will disapprove what was said in the report and Shawkey becomes a liar, the best solution was not to write the report and tells Fat'hy that it was a misunderstanding between them and he did not want to take it further. Shawkey thought of Mustafa advice, it was right, Shawkey did not want to make problems to him at work or make strong enemies like these two managers, so he returned to Fat'hy and told him that he do not want to take it further and will not write the report, Mustafa was right, suddenly Fat'hy exploded on Shawkey and told him if he did not want to take it further then why he told him about it in the first place, he told Shawkey that he do not want to hear anything from him in the future about his problems at work, it was clear that Fat'hy wanted to attack Tahsen by Shawkey's report, it was a valuable chance for him. Since that day Fat'hy started treating Shawkey in a rude way, he did not talk with him, but let Mustafa deliver the message or the tasks to him and if he spoke with Shawkey it was in a rude and rough way, also it was clear that he wanted to get rid of Shawkey and bring another Egyptian engineer a friend of him to replace Shawkey in the company, other development occurred in Iraq, the Ba'ath party office in his home area had visited his home there to ask about the whereabouts of Shawkey, his mother told them that he was working in Yemen and they told her that he should be there in Iraq serving his country instead of working abroad, Samera told Shawkey what happened by the phone, also she told him that Yemen was not a safe place for him now, because the government of Yemen was a friend of Saddam, the best solution for him was to travel to England where his father friend Mahmood lives, he was a rich man and will look after him. Shawkey started thinking of travelling to England, he prepared his travelling documents.

Shawkey had spent two and half years working with Al-sa'ed company and felt that it was the time to move on, he saw Sameha two more times at the house, but the land lord had contacted him and told him that one of the neighbours had saw females leaving the house and the house was empty most of the time, he went himself there and found no furniture or any proof that it was occupied, so he cancelled the rent and took over the flat, when Shawkey saw him and tried to convince him that he sometimes spends the nights with his friends, it did not work and he lost the flat, then he started taking Sameha outside Taiz to have sex with her at the back seat. Mahmood was a friend of Karem Shawkey's father, he was a rich man living in England , he was an engineer finished his degree in England , he had two girls and a boy, his oldest daughter her name (Aola), she had finished her master degree and looking for work, her younger sister (Adab) was still studying her master degree and the boy his name (Ali) was still studying his bachelor of science, Mahmood was an artist drawing paintings and present them in fairs he makes from time to time. When Shawkey told Mahmood of his intension to visit them in England, Mahmood encouraged him and sent him an invitation to see one of his exhibitions that he will make soon, he sent the invitation to Shawkey and a copy to the British embassy in Yemen, Shawkey added this invitation to his travel application papers to get his visa. Shawkey completed his visa and was ready to travel, at that time he asked Hamdon to buy him a ticket to England as it was required in his contract with the company, they bought him a one way ticket to England, at this time Shawkey's contract with the company had finished and Hamdon did not renew it, which proves that the decision had been made to replace Shawkey with the other Egyptian engineer (no new contract and one way ticket), Shawkey did not bother much about the matter, he wanted to go and live in England where there was safety away from the horror of Saddam and his Ba'ath party. In this last month of Shawkey's life in Yemen, he prepared himself and bought personal gold for him to wear it in the airport, so that they do not tax him in Yemen, he was allowed to carry certain amount of dollars with him, he transferred the rest of the money through an Arabic bank which had a branch in England, then he told Abani about what happened and asked her to continue corresponding with him, he took her mail box address in Taiz. About Sameha it was a painful matter to Shawkey, because he knew that she was loving him and he had feelings towards her still it was not the same feelings he felt before towards Aida, he did not know how to open the subject to her and what will be her reaction, but he must tell her as a matter of respect. In his week before the last , after he took her to the isolated place, he told her about the development at his work and his decision to travel to England, suddenly the tears started falling from her eyes, it was a painful sight, he hated himself for it, but it was too late now and everything was ready, he cannot go back, she asked him (how long you will stay in England) she asked the question without a smile, he said (I do not know, I want to settle first then decide when to come back), he knew that he was lying but he wanted to reduce the impact on her, then he told her to rent a mail box in her name, so that they can correspond with each other, she told him that she has a friend who has a mail box I can correspond with her using her friend mail box, she will take her permission and give him the address during the next week before he travel, their meeting was short and sad, in spite of Sameha's pain she kept a brave face to save her pride. At the last week he met her and she gave him the mail box address.

The day come for Shawkey to travel and leave Yemen forever, he took a taxi from Taiz to Sana'a and from Sana'a he took his flight to England.

England (1993)

Shawkey's flight was long it took eight hours, at last he got to Gatwick airport, it was April and it was raining, when he got out of the airport, Mahmood and his oldest daughter Aola were waiting for him, they welcomed him and took him by their car to their home, in the way Shawkey saw the cars moving from the left he was surprised, it was a different system of driving than the one in Yemen and Iraq, he asked them how they do that, they told him that the driving system in England was different from many countries including the Middle east, Mahmood was living in Surrey which was a nice county in England, it have many trees, their house was in Cobham which was also a posh area in Surrey occupied by rich people, his house was build on one acre of land, there was a long entrance, front and back gardens, the house itself consists of four bedrooms, two receptions, one big hall way called studio where he used to do his exhibitions or family parties, Mahmood wife and the rest of his children were waiting for Shawkey, they welcomed him for his visit and wished him a happy stay. Shawkey used to call Mahmood uncle as a matter of respect, he stayed in his house for twenty five days, during this period he used to take the trains to London and back to Surrey, Shawkey liked London very much and decided to settle in it, there were too many Iraqis living in London, he met them and told them about his wish to stay and live in England, because of the horror of Saddam, they advised him to apply for political asylum, they told him about a place called Iraqi community association where they deal with all Iraqis issues and the people there can help him. Shawkey went there; he introduced himself to them and told them about his wish, they helped him to prepare his papers and submitting it to the home office. Shawkey waited for two weeks and the result came , he had got a political asylum and has the right to remain in the UK for four years, the reason for this quick decision, because he was from Al-hakem family , which was known to the British government, Saddam had prosecuted the members of this family in many occasions. The situation of Shawkey in England was political asylum and he can ask aid from the government, he rented a small studio flat consists of one small room and bathroom, there was a small cooker, bed and a wardrobe, the flat was in a nice area in London called Bayswater, there were many Arab in the area including Iraqis, he moved to this flat and left Mahmood house. Everyday Shawkey used to see the people in the morning go to their work and he was sitting in his flat unemployed, he was feeling sad, he used to work and earn his money, one day he was sitting in one of the parks near his flat looking to the people busy with their matters and told himself (I will find a work one day, the most important thing I am here in England, the land of safety, money, freedom and sex) his eyes were looking at an English blonde female, he kept looking at her erotically until she disappeared.

www.ingramcontent.com/pod-product-compliance
Lightning Source LLC
Chambersburg PA
CBHW060224290526
45789CB00003B/1407